Dedication

I would like to dedicate this book to my wonderful family: my golfer husband, Steve, who encouraged me to pursue my dreams; my precious teenage children, Lindsay and Ryan, who gave me feedback on my material; my brothers Tom and Eric and their families, who cheered me on at the sidelines; and my friends, who love and support me, just because that's what friends do.

Table of Contents

CD Files

Project Photo Slideshows

File Folder Books
1.) The Flap Book
2.) The Dutch Door Book
3.) The Expanding Book

Grocery Bag Books
1.) The Basic Book
2.) The Panel Book
3.) The Traveling Mat Book

Lunch Bag Books
1.) The Traditional Bag Book
2.) The Pocket Guide Book
3.) The Explosion Book

Paper Books
1.) The Never-ending Book
2.) The Circle Book
3.) The Hanging Star Book

Rubrics

Amazing Literature Project Rubric A

Amazing Literature Project Rubric B

Amazing Literature Project Rubric C

Amazing Literature Project Rubric D

Sample Enrichment Handouts

Character Traits

Conflict-resolution Skills

Transforming Disaster into Humor

Sample Projects and Worksheets

Of Mice and Men Project

The Anti-Defamation League's Pyramid of Hate

The Odyssey Project

The Odyssey Project Templates

Romeo and Juliet Project

Travel Journal

Templates

Basic Book Pocket Template

Basic Book Text Box Template

Circle Book Template

Circle Book Text Box Template

Dutch Door Book Text Box Template

Templates (cont.)

Expanding Book Text Box Template

Expanding Book Text Triangle Template

Explosion Book Text Box Template

Hanging Star Book Text Box Template

Never-ending Book Text Box Template

Panel Book Pocket Template

Panel Book Text Box Template

Template for Designing Assignments

Traditional Bag Book Text Box Template

Traveling Mat Book Pocket Template

Traveling Mat Book Text Box Template

Acknowledgments

I would like to thank the outstanding Hillsborough School District in New Jersey, especially my principal, Karen Bingert, my supervisors, Maggie Taub and Carol Butler; and my gifted colleagues, who encouraged me to have students create these awe-inspiring, multi-faceted books enriched with many life lessons.

Last, I would like to thank Maupin House Publishing who believed that I had a truly innovative idea and gave me the ability to actualize my vision so that I am now able to share it with teachers and students nationwide. For this I am grateful.

Introduction

An Excellent Product-based Assessment

For learning to be highly successful, I believe any projects assigned by the teacher should be hands on and meaningful to students. Our brains learn best when they "do" rather than "absorb." It is important for teachers to help students actively display their thorough knowledge and understanding of a text in a creative and original manner.

Constructing original books offers an especially creative way for students to demonstrate their response to a literary work. Interactive literature-response keepsakes structure activities in different ways, including the use of visual, auditory, and tactile-kinesthetic modes of learning. Having these varied components in an assignment increases academic performance and improves attitudes toward learning. When students create, assemble, and present captivating and comprehensive books that implement the literary benchmarks and several critical-thinking levels, their individual voice, style, and originality are encouraged.

These are not little craft projects. They are challenging and hands on. They require students to express themselves individually and, at the same time, work toward specific language-arts objectives using Bloom's Taxonomy of higher-level critical-thinking skills, core curriculum content standards, and other enrichment features, such as life skills and technology.

This integrated approach offers students a wide range of strategies to comprehend, understand, assess, and appreciate texts. Students can respond to several rhetorical situations, addressing specific audiences for certain purposes. Additionally, by using technology, students can integrate images, art, and graphic designs to compose their responses, merging the verbal response with the visual representation.

Supplies for these interactive books are relatively inexpensive and easily available in schools: card stock, brown lunch bags, large grocery bags, or file folders. Students feel quite accomplished by producing essential responses in a compact book because these handmade wonders look so complex and impressive, yet they are incredibly simple to make. Teachers enjoy evaluating these innovative products that emphasize critical thinking, modes of writing, and artistic expression.

The projects described in this book are comprehensive, reflective, evaluative, and creative but easily accessible and dynamic . . . and isn't that what learning is all about?

How to Use This Book

PART I: SIX KEYS FOR DESIGNING AMAZING ASSIGNMENTS explains all of the strategies and tips you need to plan and design amazing literature-response projects while keeping in mind state standards, varied critical-thinking levels, supplemental texts, student supports, student choice, and a design template.

PART II: TWELVE AMAZING BOOKS TO CREATE provides step-by-step instructions, diagrams, photos, and templates for a dozen different literature-response projects that will amaze you and your students.

PART III: ASSESSING AMAZING HANDS-ON LITERATURE PROJECTS offer the rubrics and guidelines you need to grade these meaningful projects in an equally meaningful way.

SAMPLE PROJECTS AND WORKSHEETS is the final section, which includes supplemental handouts for enrichment and specific project samples for *The Odyssey, Romeo and Juliet,* and *Of Mice and Men.*

The **SUPPLEMENTAL CD** included with this book contains all the necessary project reproducibles, handouts, and rubrics. Full-color photos of all twelve projects completed by real secondary students are also included and can be shown in class to guide students from starting their projects through completion. To view photos in a slideshow format in Windows, simply open the folder with the photos, go to the View menu, select "Filmstrip," and click the arrows to move from photo to photo, step by step.

Objectives for *Amazing Hands-On Literature Projects for Secondary Students*

Students will:

- meet state core curriculum content standards;
- develop and apply different levels of critical thinking according to Bloom's Taxonomy so that they comprehend, analyze, and create new materials;
- read, analyze, and synthesize information from multiple sources such as editorials, historical texts, maps, and more;
- use multiple intelligences to understand a text;
- experiment with different forms of writing such as newspaper articles, letters, and essays;
- consider purpose, audience, and tone in writing;
- receive differentiated instruction and be given choices based on their specific needs; and
- follow oral and written directions to create a handmade keepsake book as response to a literary work.

Designing Amazing Assignments

When you select a text, begin thinking about it in broader terms. Ask yourself what concepts you want students to preserve not only this year but also in their lives. A great place to start is to examine your state's core standards. These serve as a foundation for purposeful assignments.

Next, decide the number and types of assignments you want to create. Based on that, generate three different levels of critical-thinking assignments. Start with the foundational level; these are concrete questions based on knowledge and comprehension. Then move to the analytical level, which poses investigative questions that require higher-level thinking skills—the *how* and the *why*. The third and most challenging level is the transformational level. Here, students synthesize and evaluate the text through creating, combining, and assessing.

In addition to the assignment itself, you should consider distributing several short non-fiction or fiction supplemental works at the beginning of and throughout the reading of the text. These help emphasize themes found in the main work, such as current teen issues a character shares with students, conflict-resolution strategies, or character education. Having students make connections with the original text, these outside works, and their lives is a crucial part of the literature project.

When designing amazing assignments, often teachers want to push students out of their comfort zones. In order for students to be successful, teachers may need to provide frameworks prior to beginning a particular assignment. These scaffolds fall into three categories: content, writing, and communication. These scaffolds and all of the design strategies are explained further in **Part I: Six Keys for Designing Amazing Assignments**.

After you have decided the number and variety of responses your project will contain and which way your students will accomplish the designated tasks, select the type of keepsake to accommodate your agenda. It's best to start with a simple book such as the Traditional Bag Book.

You can then work your way up to more challenging projects. Remember: It's your book, your project, your way.

Classroom Management Tips

Designing your questions based on critical-thinking level and purpose takes much preparation. However, once you generate your assignments, you can organize and distribute the material easily with your timetable in mind.

At the start of each unit, let students know to save all their work because it will be compiled into a handmade book. To begin, you can give supplemental reading and research-based questions that students can complete for homework. Consider designing a template for the assigned work that students can download and complete to fit into the space in the handmade book. Then, as the class is reading, provide both foundational and analytical questions. Toward the conclusion of the unit, provide transformational questions.

Once the reading is finished, set aside one or two class periods to make the actual handmade book. During this time, have students cut the bags and paper and assemble the actual keepsake. For a week thereafter, students can use their time to complete their content requirements for the book. They can answer the remaining questions alone, in groups, or guided by you if necessary. They can work in the computer lab or in the classroom. Allow time for students to decorate the book at home so it truly can be amazing and reinforce all the concepts stressed in the project. Finally, have a show-and-tell day when students orally present their responses to the class.

To ensure that your project runs successfully, have a checklist of assignments with specific, intermittent due dates. Many students can handle long-term projects; however, some students are not good planners and need to be held accountable frequently. If the project is due all at once, these students often leave the work to the last minute and submit incomplete or careless work.

Most students love these amazing projects. However, if you meet resistant students, have them write their responses in a report format and add simple clip art for each response. Remember, the most important component in their projects is the quality of the response.

Using Technology to Create and Access Assignments

It may be a significant amount of work to place all assignments and templates on your school website or wiki for students to access and complete at school and/or home. However, in the long run, this advanced organization will cut down on much time and confusion.

Grading Projects

When students know what is expected of them, they strive to reach those goals. Therefore, it is important to let your students know beforehand exactly what makes a good final product and why. In fact, many experts believe using assessment rubrics to measure students' work is more valuable than assigning a single numerical score because students' performances are based on the sum of a full range of criteria (Andrade). Rubrics especially match the comprehensive nature of these literature projects.

Decide what criteria you would like to employ for grading. Students can be evaluated on the following features: requirements, sources, content, organization, conventions, design, and creativity. Grading values can range from superior mastery to poor performance. You will enjoy seeing the effort, creativity, and thought that went into your students' projects as much as they enjoyed making them.

PART 1

SIX KEYS FOR DESIGNING AMAZING ASSIGNMENTS

KEY 1 Use state standards and benchmarks to generate essential questions for amazing assignments.

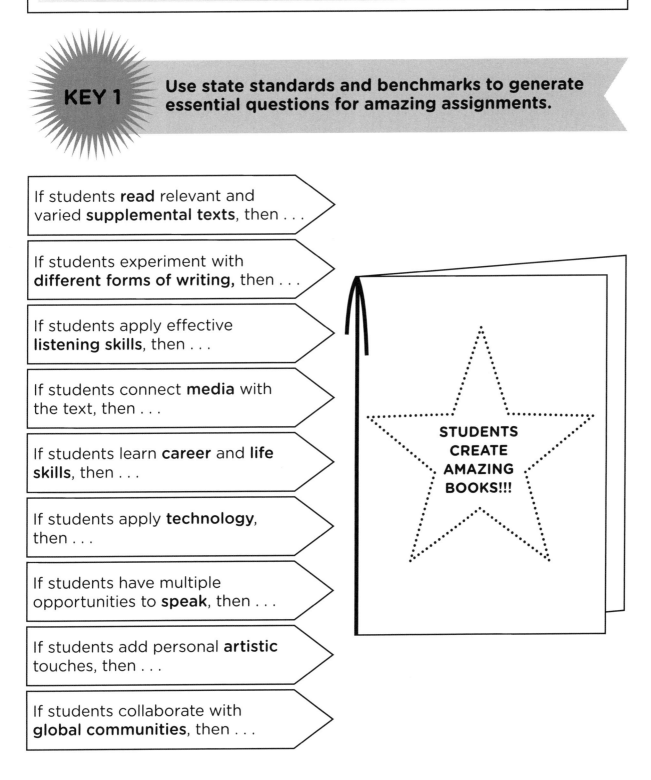

If students **read** relevant and varied **supplemental texts,** then . . .

If students experiment with **different forms of writing,** then . . .

If students apply effective **listening skills,** then . . .

If students connect **media** with the text, then . . .

If students learn **career** and **life skills,** then . . .

If students apply **technology,** then . . .

If students have multiple opportunities to **speak,** then . . .

If students add personal **artistic** touches, then . . .

If students collaborate with **global communities,** then . . .

STUDENTS CREATE AMAZING BOOKS!!!

As explained in the introduction, a great way to decide on the goals and objectives for each project is by examining state standards and benchmarks. Doing so will help ensure that you comply with state mandates and generate purposeful assignments.

An *amazing* literature project incorporates several standards to enhance learning. Recently, my state of New Jersey has urged teachers to incorporate not only language-arts standards, but also visual arts; career education and consumer, family, and life skills; technological literacy; and 21st-century standards.

By integrating a number of benchmarks, the projects in this book offer students richer perspectives on their world and an understanding of the complexities that exist. They also allow students to explore and apply life skills to address these complexities. For example, students can apply the given course content to investigate career issues of their choosing; they can learn to apply important life skills such as problem solving with win-win outcomes; and they can expand their vision to include the world beyond their school or town. What is most wonderful about this approach is that students can create handmade keepsakes that they can refer to months or years later, thereby reinforcing the course material well after the course has ended!

The following is an overview of the state benchmarks incorporated into *Amazing Hands-On Literature Projects for Secondary Students*. I used New Jersey standards as a model, but most states include the same objectives and cumulative progress indicators. However, the configuration may vary from state to state. Again, it is recommended teachers briefly examine the state standards that follow to understand the total scope of the project.

An Integration of State Standards

General Standard	Students will . . .
Reading	• read a variety of texts for fluency and comprehension.
	• use many opportunities to think about, talk about, and write about the texts they are reading in order to grow as readers and deepen their understanding of texts.
	• read a diversity of material (including fiction and non-fiction) in order to provide students with opportunities to grow intellectually, emotionally, and socially as they consider universal themes, diverse cultures and perspectives, and the common aspects of human existence.
	• respond to texts, both personally and critically, and relate prior knowledge and personal experiences to written texts.
	• apply literal, inferential, and critical comprehension strategies before, during, and after reading to examine, construct, and extend meaning.

Writing

- write in clear, concise, organized language that varies in content and form for different audiences, purpose, and tone with consideration for composition, communication, expression, learning, and engaging the reader.
- learn a repertoire of strategies to enable them to vary form, style, and conventions.
- have multiple opportunities to craft and practice writing, to generate ideas and to refine, evaluate, and publish their writing.
- develop and demonstrate fluency in all phases of the writing process, including pre-writing, drafting, revising, editing of multiple drafts, and post-writing processes that include publishing, presenting, and evaluating.
- understand the recursive nature and shifting perspectives of the writing process, in moving from the role of writer to the role of reader and back again.
- learn to appreciate writing not only as a product, but also as a process and mode of thinking and communicating.

Speaking

- recognize that what they hear, write, read, and view contributes to the content and quality of their oral language.
- speak in clear, concise, organized language that varies in content and form for different audiences, purpose, and tone.
- organize and deliver information clearly and adapt to their listeners in order to express, transmit, and exchange information, ideas, and emotions.
- have multiple opportunities to share their creations in and outside the classroom setting.

Listening

- understand that listening is the process of hearing, receiving, constructing meaning from, and responding to spoken and/or nonverbal messages.
- require different listening skills to actively listen to information from a variety of sources in a variety of situations, such as comprehending information or evaluating a message.
- gain understanding and appreciation of language and communication by active listening.
- apply effective listening skills, such as listening actively, restating, interpreting, responding to, and evaluating increasingly complex messages, such as following directions to create a product.

Viewing and Media Literacy	• comprehend and respond to personal interactions, live performances, visual arts that involve oral and/or written language, and both print media (graphs, charts, diagrams, illustrations, photographs, and graphic design in books, magazines, and newspapers) and electronic media (television, computers, and film).
	• understand that messages are representations of social reality and vary by historic time periods and parts of the world.
	• evaluate media for credibility and understand how words, images, and sounds influence the way meanings are conveyed and understood in contemporary society.
Visual and Performing Arts	• develop a capacity to perceive and respond imaginatively to our world.
	• experiment with various forms of artistic expression.
	• acquire knowledge and skills that contribute to aesthetic awareness of the arts in order to strengthen our appreciation of the world, as well as our abilities to be creative and inventive.
Career Education and Consumer, Family, and Life Skills	• develop consumer, family, and life skills necessary to be functioning members of society.
	• recognize problems, devise a variety of ways to solve these problems, analyze the potential advantages and disadvantages of each alternative, and evaluate the effectiveness of the method ultimately selected.
	• work collaboratively with a variety of groups and demonstrate the essential components of character development and ethics, including trustworthiness, responsibility, respect, fairness, caring, and citizenship.
	• apply principles of resource management and skills that promote personal and professional well-being, such as wellness, child development, and human relationships.
Technological Literacy	• use computer applications and technology to conduct research, solve problems, improve learning, achieve goals, and produce products and presentations.
	• develop, locate, summarize, organize, synthesize, and evaluate information for lifelong learning.
	• develop an understanding of the nature and impact of technology, engineering, technological design, and the designed world as they relate to the individual, society, and the environment.

21ˢᵗ-century Standards (Global)

- choose a wide range of readings to enhance their understanding of the text and their world.

- build relationships with others to pose and solve problems collaboratively and cross-culturally.

- design and share information for global communities to meet for a variety of purposes.

- manage, analyze, and synthesize multiple streams of simultaneous information to create and communicate knowledge.

- attend to ethical responsibilities required by these complex environments.

(Adapted from NCTE Definition of 21st Century Literacies 2008)

Condensed from *New Jersey Core Curriculum Standards*, NJ Department of Education

KEY 2 Craft assignments based on critical-thinking levels progressing from simplest to most complex.

Based on Bloom's goals for the educational process, teachers should design project assignments that include a range of cognitive objectives that move from the simplest critical-thinking tasks to the most complex. Loren Anderson, a former student of Bloom, revisited this cognitive domain during the 1990s and made some changes to subdivide the cognitive process into the six classifications explained in this section (Clark, 2009).

I chose to modify Bloom's/Anderson's Taxonomy into three cognitive-level groupings. The first is the **foundational** level, which includes the two primary categories of cognitive-thinking skills. This simplest level includes tasks such as recalling, basic understanding, and interpreting. The second is the **analytical** level, which includes the middle two tiers on Bloom's cognitive scale. At this stage, a more complex intellectual skill level is required. Students are required to apply skills, recognize patterns, and break down information into parts. The third level is the **transformational** level, which has the highest educational goal. This most complex tier aims to challenge kids to evaluate texts and create new products.

Use All Three Critical-thinking Levels

COGNITIVE LEVEL	RANGE OF DIFFICULTY	TASK CLASSIFICATION
Level 1: Foundational	Simplest	Remembering/Understanding
Level 2: Analytical	Complex	Applying/Analyzing
Level 3: Transformational	Most Complex	Evaluating/Creating

Use Product-based Verbs

The following is a list of action verbs classified by cognitive ability. When you design assignments for a project, you should incorporate tasks from all three levels. When choosing tasks for Levels 1 and 2, there may be an equal distribution of assignments from simple to moderately complex. However, since Level 3 requires the most rigorous cognitive thinking, there should be fewer assignments generated from this category.

Level 1 Foundational		Level 2 Analytical		Level 3 Transformational	
Remembering	**Understanding**	**Applying**	**Analyzing**	**Evaluating**	**Creating**
choose	approximate	adapt	analyze	agree	anticipate
circle	cite	alter	ask	appraise	assemble
count	characterize	answer	break down	argue	combine
describe	clarify	apply	categorize	assess	compare
define	conclude	assess	chart	choose	compile
draw	compare	change	classify	compare	connect
find	define	chart	compare	conclude	construct
how	demonstrate	choose	contrast	consider	create
identify	describe	construct	correlate	contrast	design
know	discuss	demonstrate	deduce	criticize	develop
label	distinguish	determine	diagram	decide	devise
list	explain	develop	differentiate	debate	establish
locate	express	discover	discriminate	defend	express
match	generalize	draw	distinguish	determine	generate
name	give examples	establish	divide	discriminate	graph
quote	identify	extend	document	editorialize	hypothesize
outline	illustrate	generalize	examine	evaluate	imagine
pick	interpret	illustrate	explain	explain	invent
recall	locate	inform	identify	give opinion	judge
recognize	make sense	interview	illustrate	influence	make
record	observe	investigate	infer	interpret	make up
select	paraphrase	organize	inquire	judge	modify
sequence	predict	place	observe	justify	organize
state	relate	predict	order	predict	originate

(Adapted from Bloom's/Anderson's Taxonomy Verbs)

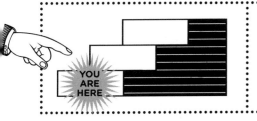

Amazing Assignments Level 1
FOUNDATIONAL

Compose a personal journal entry about an event that took place in the text.

Construct a timeline.

Create a dossier on a character. Pretend to be a foreign spy; gather specific information and a photo.

Create a process/cycle diagram.

Create a scale diagram.

Create an informational pamphlet.

Define literary elements.

Describe a setting using spatial-order transitions.

Design a travel brochure or town tour.

Draw a character, a setting, or an aspect of the book.

Draw a map of the setting or physical movements of a character.

Draw a picture of a significant event.

Explain a process.

Find a recipe of a common food during the book's time period.

Give a character sketch.

Locate setting in the text and print a map using an electronic source.

Locate literary elements in the text.

Make a collage.

Make a T-chart.

Offer background information on transportation, fashion, food, customs, religious practices, or government from the time period in the text.

Plot events using Freytag's Pyramid.

Recount the story using the five W's and H.

Research an author and compose the text for the book jacket.

Research the historical period of the text.

Research the meaning of five characters' names. Explain why they are suitable for each character.

Sequence the events in a story.

Summarize the plot.

Trace one character's movements.

Write five quotes from the text and explain their meanings.

Write an observation report.

Write the title of the book down the side of the paper. For each letter, construct a meaningful sentence that begins with each letter (acrostic).

Analyze a theme.

Analyze cause/effect relationships.

Apply the Anti-Defamation League's Pyramid of Hate to the text and locate examples of discrimination.

Apply research to text: anthropology, biology, history, political science, psychology, and sociology.

Chart the emotional growth of a character.

Compare and contrast one character to a person in contemporary society.

Compare and contrast the text with film.

Compare and contrast two characters.

Compare youth in the text with youth of today.

Complete a police report about an incident in the text.

Consider which national organizations a character would support.

Create a postcard from a character about an event.

Create an obituary for a character.

Create and present a collage of words and images from the book.

Decide which astrological sign a character was born under based on his/her personality traits.

Describe a chat room a character would choose to enter.

Describe a problem and offer a better solution than the one given in the book.

Design a scrapbook page for your character and include meaningful events or people.

Discuss a tragic flaw in one character's personality that leads to trouble.

Establish cause-and-effect relationships.

Explain five themes.

Explain a character's choice of a vacation destination.

Explain the author's word choice and meaning.

Explain qualities of heroism in a character.

Have a character send a letter to someone about a concern: personal, business, professional, editorial, or complaint.

Have a victim bring another character to justice in a public forum.

Identify problems and solutions.

Interview a character and ask probing questions. Answer the questions in the character's persona.

List three gifts you would give the main characters and why.

Locate current events that reflect incidents in the book.

Locate literary devices and purpose.

Nominate a character for a specific award.

Prosecute a character for a crime/injustice.

Psychoanalyze a character and offer a prognosis.

Research and apply a medical/psychological diagnosis to a character.

Research the "Pillars of Character." Examine the book for characters who exhibit these traits.

Select five lines of text and explain their significance.

Send an e-mail from one character to another concerning an event in the text.

Think about what occupations are most suitable for a character and why.

Write a letter to the author.

Write a medical lab report based on an incident in the text.

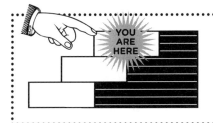

YOU ARE HERE

Amazing Assignments Level 3
TRANSFORMATIONAL

Analyze a crime scene. Write a coroner's report.

Apply five proverbs to characters in the book. Explain why they relate to that person.

Compose a bad news letter to/from a character.

Compose a book review for Oprah's Book Club.

Compose a protest letter for a real or fictitious government official.

Craft a public service announcement making people aware of a social, health, or school issue.

Create a front-page news story.

Create a parody of the work.

Create a speech a character could give on a national issue that reflects that person's personality and beliefs.

Create an advertisement for a specific historical time period.

Create an online profile for a character on Facebook.

Create bumper stickers for each character.

Design a book jacket.

Design a theme park ride based on one aspect of the book.

Design a T-shirt based on an aspect of the book.

Design a webpage for a character.

Develop a "wanted" poster that gives a character description, offenses, other pertinent information, and a reward.

Develop an advice column from Dr. Phil.

Draw an editorial cartoon.

Evaluate choices made by characters.

Generate a new chapter for the book. Consider before the book began, shortly after the ending of the book, or several years later.

Have a victim press charges against a character or the state. What is the complaint/outcome?

Host an intervention. What advice would each person give the main character?

Imagine if a character lived in the present day. What clothes, books, movies, and activities would that person prefer?

Imagine a character lived in another time period. Describe the problems that would arise for the character and the outcomes.

List a character's personal item on eBay. What is the asking price and actual selling price, and who buys it?

List ten songs a character would have on his/her iPod.

List the top ten websites a character would go to.

Mimic the author's style in a song (i.e., transform a rap song into the writing style of the author).

Research and apply a medical/psychological diagnosis to the character.

Roast a character.

Trade places with a character from the book. Explain why you would/would not like doing so.

Transform a humorous scene into a serious one.

Transform a serious scene into a comedic one.

Write a bill or bylaw. Give support for its enforcement.

Write a congratulatory letter to a character from a real or imagined person.

Write a report as a social worker on the conditions of the home or life of a character in the book.

Write a résumé for a character.

Write a sales script for the book.

Write a segment of the story from a different point of view.

Write an original poem or song.

KEY 3 — Choose supplemental readings to enhance the learning experience.

If students are to create amazing projects, teachers should not only include what is academically essential for the students to acquire in the classroom, but also what is essential for enhancing students' lives.

One 21st-century standard suggests that students should read a wide range of print and non-print texts in order to build an understanding of a text, of themselves, and of cultures of the United States and the world. By providing supplemental readings, teachers expose students to new ideas and keep them up to date on current trends and issues so that they can respond successfully to the requirements and demands of our culture.

In addition, by adding enrichment texts, teachers foster in students a deeper understanding of the human experience. Through provided readings, students gain necessary life skills, make connections with their environment, and develop an awareness of the complexities that exist in our world.

Assigning supplemental texts allows students to use a variety of technological and scholarly resources, as well. Students can collect an infinite amount of information expediently, organize it, and even transform it to create a new product.

Supplemental Enrichment Text Topics

NON-FICTON	NON-FICTON	FICTION
Anthropology	Life skills	Comics
Arts	Lifestyle and culture	Films
Biographies and memoirs	Literary terms	Plays
Business and investing	Literary criticism	Poems
Character education/traits	Magazine articles	Short stories
Charts	Medical	
Civics	Mental health	
Computer and Internet	Natural history	
Cooking	Newspapers	
Crafts and hobbies	Outdoors and nature	
Crime and criminals	Parenting and family	
Current events	Philosophy	
Diagrams	Photography	
Dictionaries	Politics	
Diversity	Professional and technical	
Documentary film	Psychological texts	
Economics	Reference	

NON-FICTON (CONT.)

Encyclopedias

Essays on topic

Forensic articles

Genealogy

Government

Graphs

Health, mind, and body

History

How-to articles

Law

Letters and correspondence

NON-FICTON (CONT.)

Social sciences

Social issues

Science self-help guides

Sociology

School

Sports

Teens

Travel

True accounts

Urban planning/development

Women's studies

KEY 4 Provide necessary supports for students to execute project tasks.

Planning amazing projects also requires teachers to look ahead and anticipate what students may need to accomplish the tasks at hand. Teachers may need to provide frameworks prior to beginning particular assignments. For example, students may need to be exposed to new subject matter, may need graphic organizers for writing structures, or may need advice on word choice and phrasing for effective communication. The three areas of assistance are content, writing, and communication.

Categories of Supports

What kind of scaffolding should teachers provide for students to execute the assignment successfully?

CONTENT SCAFFOLDS

What additional **concepts**, **terms**, or **subject matter** do the students need in order to complete the assignments?

WRITING SCAFFOLDS

What specific forms or frameworks do students require in order accomplish a particular writing assignment?

COMMUNICATION SCAFFOLDS

What skills or strategies can students use to **communicate** their ideas with more impact?

Providing Supports for Content

When designing a unit of study, teachers must remember that students come from developmentally, environmentally, and experientially diverse settings. Therefore, it is important in the planning stages for teachers to decide on which aspects of the text they wish to focus and what supports are necessary for students to grasp foreign concepts. Instructors may need to make unfamiliar subject matter clear in order for students to complete the assignment.

For instance, teachers may give an assignment to transform a serious text into a comedy, but students may not be aware of the characteristics of humor. For this reason, teachers should offer information about the elements of comedy before students begin their transformational writing.

Another situation teachers may encounter is students not having prior knowledge about issues within a text. Let's say a character is a *juvenile delinquent*. Defining the term and offering relevant examples to the students in advance would clarify this issue for students.

Also, students may not have prior knowledge about a historical event such as the Vietnam War. Teachers can furnish background material to help student make sense of their task.

Providing Supports for Writing

Students need to arrange their ideas in a set structure so that they are clear and easy to follow. Since students can be unaware of how to integrate diverse elements, they often digress in their thought patterns and may require assistance in bridging relationships between ideas.

The teacher's mission is to instruct students on how to make logical sense of these diverse elements prior to the assignment. You may want to introduce student to various forms of writing, each having its own particular purpose and distinct structure. Additionally, you may wish to employ explicit graphic organizers or outlines. Providing lessons on structure, developing and arranging ideas, and linking thoughts effectively by using specific transitions are crucial.

For instance, students may be presented with the challenge of writing a news story based on their reading. This writing technique may be alien to them, so you must explain the pattern of a news story and provide models prior to asking students to complete the task.

Also, you may require students to use direct quotes and cite their sources in their assignments. Devise a lesson that demonstrates effective use of quotations in writing so that students know beforehand how to do so.

Providing Supports for Communication

Students are asked to write for many audiences. They have much to share, but they may not know how to use words effectively. At the start of the assignment, teachers can model effective ways students can convey their ideas.

Accuracy in language usage is one communication skill students must master. They need to understand their audience and employ an appropriate tone. Therefore, lessons on word choice and sentence structure are essential.

Your goal is twofold: to have students write clearly and use lively language. You may need to dedicate class sessions to teach sentence fluency. For instance, instruct students to communicate effectively by using parallel structure that gives a rhythm to students' responses.

Another effective strategy for delivering ideas with excitement is to vary the length of sentences. Have students experiment with voice and explain how voice is what illuminates students' own unique personal tones or feelings so that it comes across in a piece of writing—replacing a stale formula. For instance, if a student is writing a persuasive letter to the board of education to allow teens to have a longer summer vacation, you could demonstrate how using precise words gets the best results.

Making choices about the mode of communication is also important. You may need to instruct students on how specific mediums—from visual to verbal to written—operate and how to evaluate which is most effective in sending their message. Overall, it is your responsibility to show students how to position their ideas successfully to have the most powerful impact.

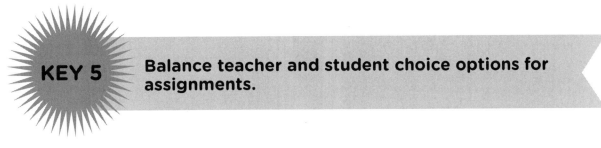

KEY 5 — Balance teacher and student choice options for assignments.

It's all about the choices! When the time comes to select the assignments for the project, provide a balance between teacher-assigned and student-selected tasks based on content standards and the three levels of critical-thinking skills.

In planning the project, you should also consider how assignments need to be accomplished. Ask yourself if certain tasks are better suited for specific groupings of individuals. Should you set up pairs, have students work independently, or address the class as a whole?

The following is a guide to assist teachers in their options for assignments.

Teachers can . . .

- design and select **all** assignments from all three levels.
- select **some** assignments for students and allow students to choose **some** assignments.
- select specific assignments to be completed in school and others to be completed for **homework**.
- allow students to choose assignments from **tiered menus**.
- allow students to work **independently**, in **pairs**, in **groups**, or as a **whole class** for specified assignments.

KEY 6

Put it all together with a template for designing assignments.

THREE CRITICAL-THINKING LEVELS 1: Foundational 2: Analytical 3: Transformational	LIST OF ASSIGNMENTS FOR THE AMAZING PROJECT (Align with state curriculum standards and 21st-century standards)	READING, WRITING, AND COMMUNICATION SUPPORTS NEEDED (Classroom instruction on making inferences, using quotations, structuring paragraphs, revising, etc.)	SUPPLEMENTAL READING APPLICATION (Research, social issues, laws, life skills, etc.)	VISUAL RESPONSE REQUIRED (Artwork, clip art, or drawings)	TYPE OF CLASSROOM INSTRUCTION (Whole class, small groups, pairs, or independent)
1	1.				
1	2.				
1	3.				
2	4.				
2	5.				
2	6.				
3	7.				
3	8.				

PART 2

TWELVE AMAZING BOOKS TO CREATE

The Traditional Bag Book

Supplies

Four or more lunch bags

Six sheets of 8 ½ × 11-in. colored card stock

  two sheets color 1 (blue)

  two sheets color 2 (green)

  two sheets color 3 (yellow)

1-in. circle punch

White school glue

Glue stick

Scissors or paper cutter

Ruler

Stapler

The Traditional Bag Book

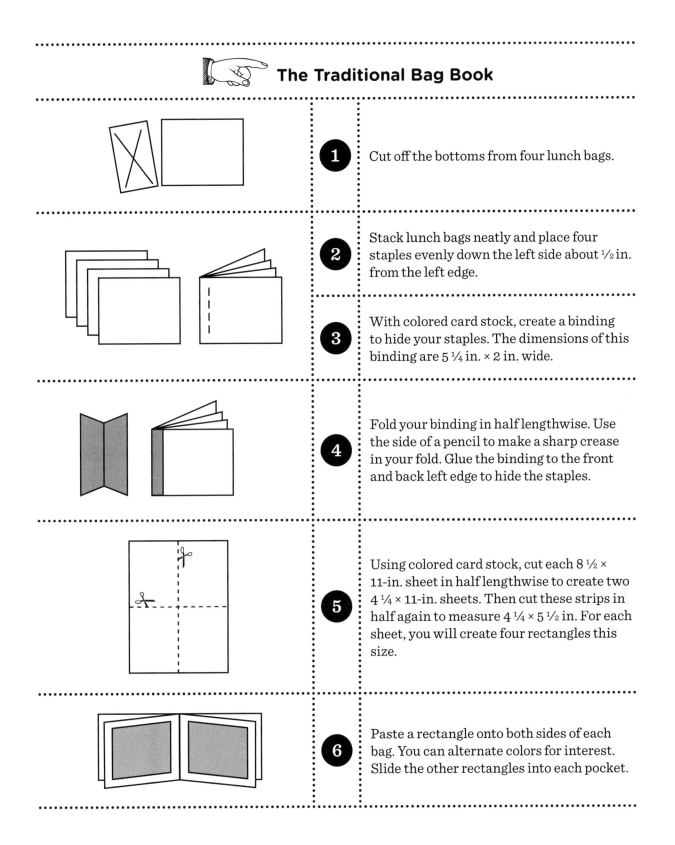

1 Cut off the bottoms from four lunch bags.

2 Stack lunch bags neatly and place four staples evenly down the left side about ½ in. from the left edge.

3 With colored card stock, create a binding to hide your staples. The dimensions of this binding are 5 ¼ in. × 2 in. wide.

4 Fold your binding in half lengthwise. Use the side of a pencil to make a sharp crease in your fold. Glue the binding to the front and back left edge to hide the staples.

5 Using colored card stock, cut each 8 ½ × 11-in. sheet in half lengthwise to create two 4 ¼ × 11-in. sheets. Then cut these strips in half again to measure 4 ¼ × 5 ½ in. For each sheet, you will create four rectangles this size.

6 Paste a rectangle onto both sides of each bag. You can alternate colors for interest. Slide the other rectangles into each pocket.

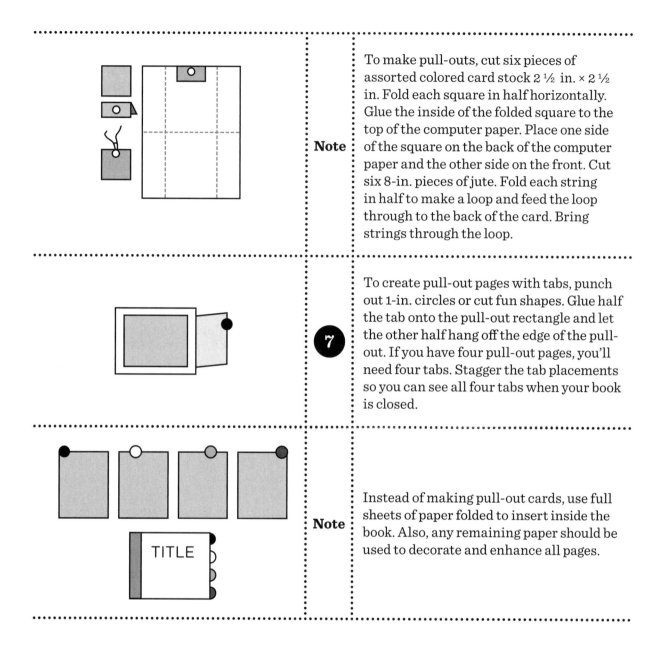

Note

To make pull-outs, cut six pieces of assorted colored card stock 2 ½ in. × 2 ½ in. Fold each square in half horizontally. Glue the inside of the folded square to the top of the computer paper. Place one side of the square on the back of the computer paper and the other side on the front. Cut six 8-in. pieces of jute. Fold each string in half to make a loop and feed the loop through to the back of the card. Bring strings through the loop.

7

To create pull-out pages with tabs, punch out 1-in. circles or cut fun shapes. Glue half the tab onto the pull-out rectangle and let the other half hang off the edge of the pull-out. If you have four pull-out pages, you'll need four tabs. Stagger the tab placements so you can see all four tabs when your book is closed.

Note

Instead of making pull-out cards, use full sheets of paper folded to insert inside the book. Also, any remaining paper should be used to decorate and enhance all pages.

Traditional Bag Book Text Box Template

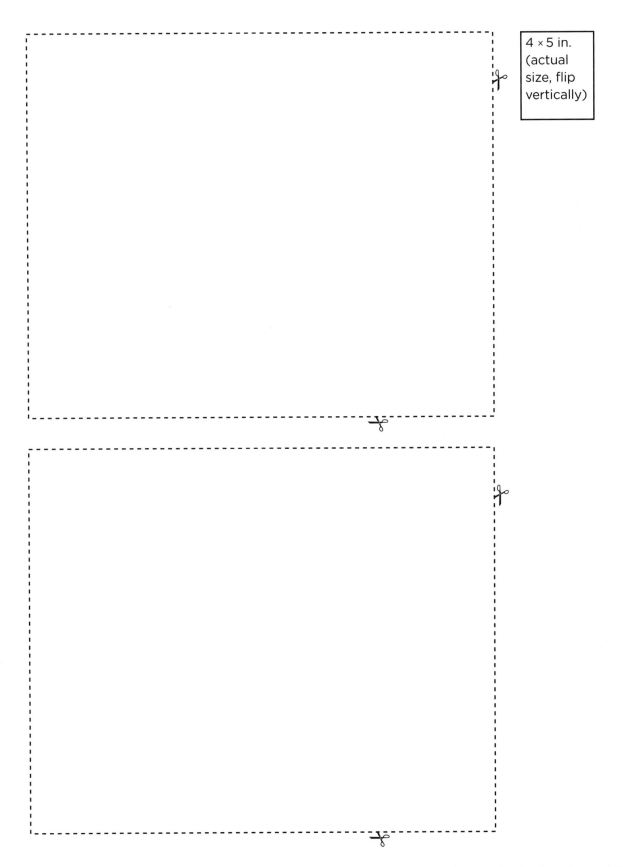

4 × 5 in.
(actual
size, flip
vertically)

The Pocket Guide Book

Supplies

Four lunch bags

Three sheets of 8½ × 11-in. assorted colored card stock

Six sheets of 8½ × 11-in. assorted colored computer paper on which to place information

White glue

Glue stick

2 yards of jute

Hole punch

The Pocket Guide Book

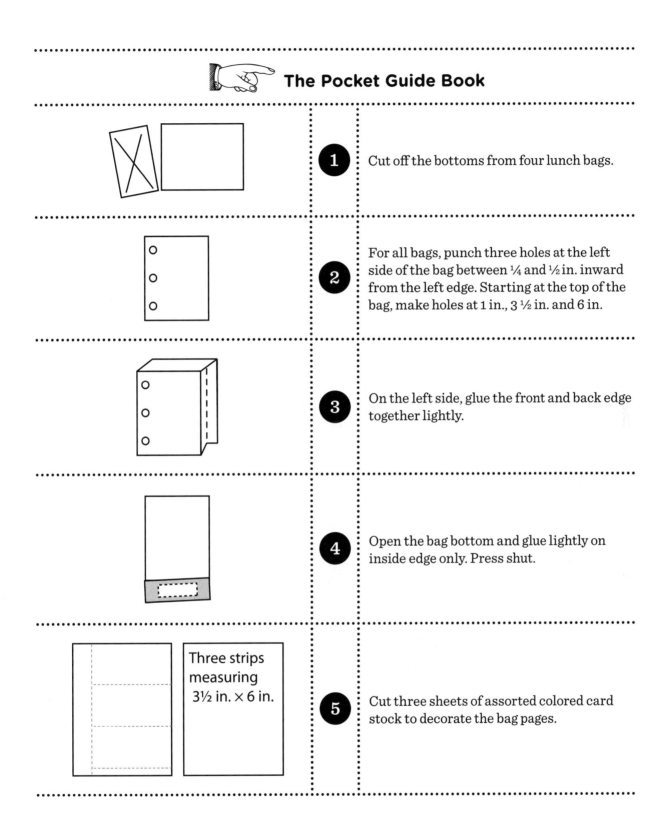

1   Cut off the bottoms from four lunch bags.

2   For all bags, punch three holes at the left side of the bag between ¼ and ½ in. inward from the left edge. Starting at the top of the bag, make holes at 1 in., 3 ½ in. and 6 in.

3   On the left side, glue the front and back edge together lightly.

4   Open the bag bottom and glue lightly on inside edge only. Press shut.

Three strips measuring 3½ in. × 6 in.

5   Cut three sheets of assorted colored card stock to decorate the bag pages.

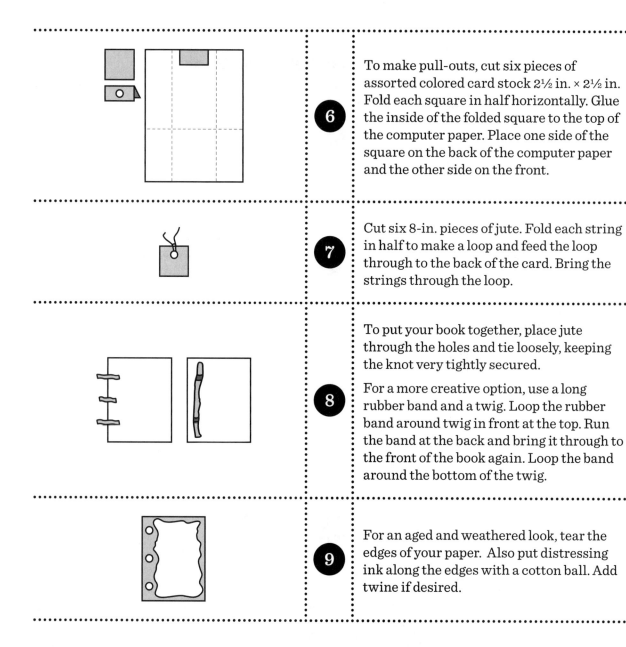

6 To make pull-outs, cut six pieces of assorted colored card stock 2½ in. × 2½ in. Fold each square in half horizontally. Glue the inside of the folded square to the top of the computer paper. Place one side of the square on the back of the computer paper and the other side on the front.

7 Cut six 8-in. pieces of jute. Fold each string in half to make a loop and feed the loop through to the back of the card. Bring the strings through the loop.

8 To put your book together, place jute through the holes and tie loosely, keeping the knot very tightly secured.

For a more creative option, use a long rubber band and a twig. Loop the rubber band around twig in front at the top. Run the band at the back and bring it through to the front of the book again. Loop the band around the bottom of the twig.

9 For an aged and weathered look, tear the edges of your paper. Also put distressing ink along the edges with a cotton ball. Add twine if desired.

The Explosion Book

Supplies

Four paper lunch bags

Scissors or paper cutter

Glue stick

White school glue

Circle punch

Roll of 2-in. packing tape (brown or clear)

1 yard of twine

Card stock cut into 4 ¼-in. squares

> three 8 ½ × 11-in sheets of color 1 (blue)
>
> three 8 ½ × 11-in sheets of color 2 (red)
>
> three 8 ½ × 11-in sheets of color 3 (yellow)

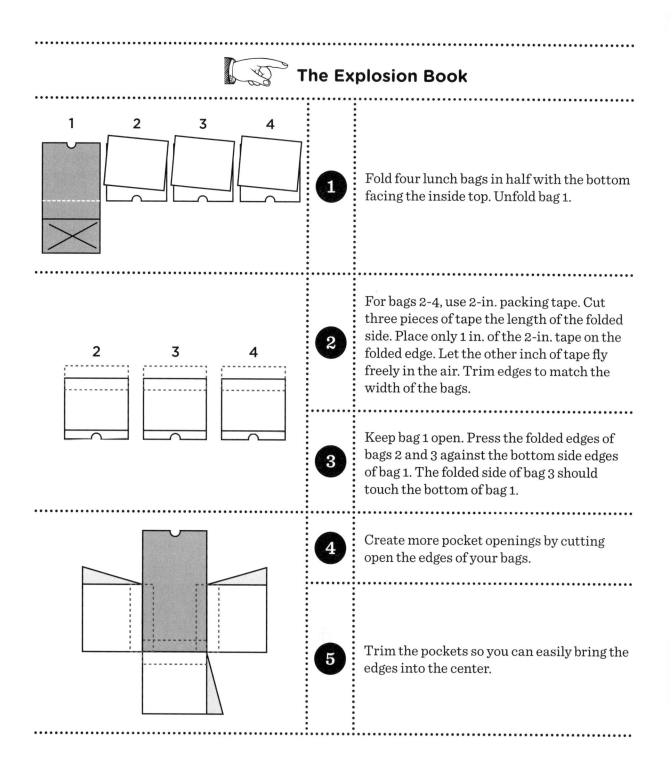

1. Fold four lunch bags in half with the bottom facing the inside top. Unfold bag 1.

2. For bags 2-4, use 2-in. packing tape. Cut three pieces of tape the length of the folded side. Place only 1 in. of the 2-in. tape on the folded edge. Let the other inch of tape fly freely in the air. Trim edges to match the width of the bags.

3. Keep bag 1 open. Press the folded edges of bags 2 and 3 against the bottom side edges of bag 1. The folded side of bag 3 should touch the bottom of bag 1.

4. Create more pocket openings by cutting open the edges of your bags.

5. Trim the pockets so you can easily bring the edges into the center.

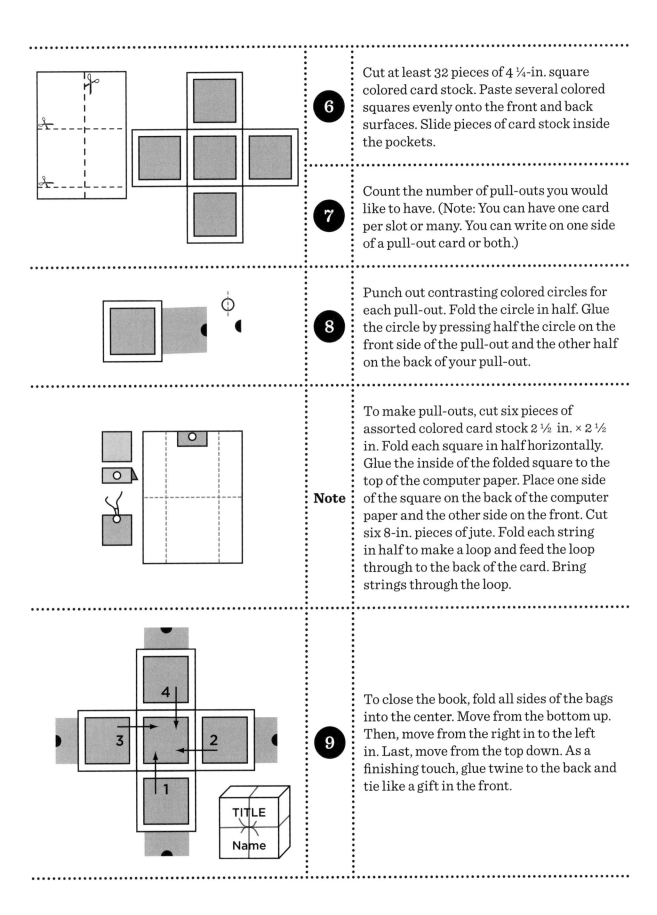

6 Cut at least 32 pieces of 4 ¼-in. square colored card stock. Paste several colored squares evenly onto the front and back surfaces. Slide pieces of card stock inside the pockets.

7 Count the number of pull-outs you would like to have. (Note: You can have one card per slot or many. You can write on one side of a pull-out card or both.)

8 Punch out contrasting colored circles for each pull-out. Fold the circle in half. Glue the circle by pressing half the circle on the front side of the pull-out and the other half on the back of your pull-out.

Note To make pull-outs, cut six pieces of assorted colored card stock 2 ½ in. × 2 ½ in. Fold each square in half horizontally. Glue the inside of the folded square to the top of the computer paper. Place one side of the square on the back of the computer paper and the other side on the front. Cut six 8-in. pieces of jute. Fold each string in half to make a loop and feed the loop through to the back of the card. Bring strings through the loop.

9 To close the book, fold all sides of the bags into the center. Move from the bottom up. Then, move from the right in to the left in. Last, move from the top down. As a finishing touch, glue twine to the back and tie like a gift in the front.

Explosion Book Text Box Template

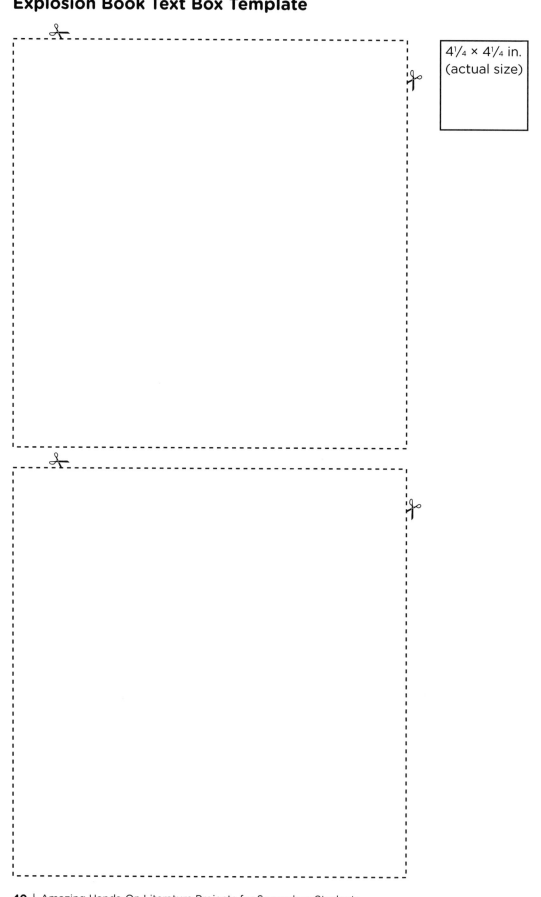

4¼ × 4¼ in. (actual size)

Grocery Bag Books

The Basic Book

Supplies

One grocery bag

White school glue

Glue stick

12-in. ruler

Scissors or paper cutter

1 yard of twine

Ten pieces of computer paper or card stock on which to place information

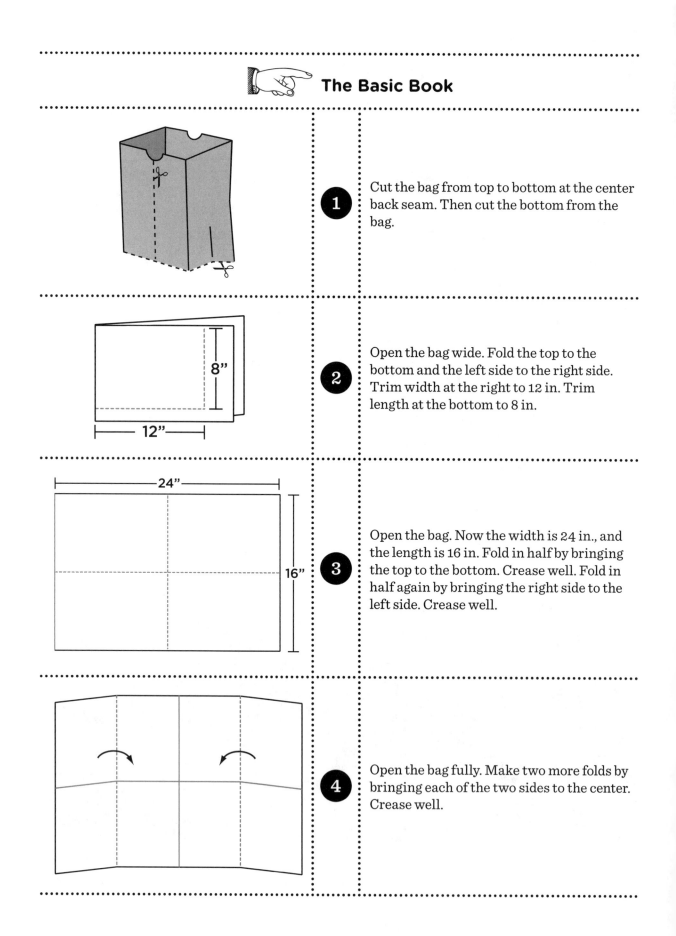

The Basic Book

1 Cut the bag from top to bottom at the center back seam. Then cut the bottom from the bag.

2 Open the bag wide. Fold the top to the bottom and the left side to the right side. Trim width at the right to 12 in. Trim length at the bottom to 8 in.

3 Open the bag. Now the width is 24 in., and the length is 16 in. Fold in half by bringing the top to the bottom. Crease well. Fold in half again by bringing the right side to the left side. Crease well.

4 Open the bag fully. Make two more folds by bringing each of the two sides to the center. Crease well.

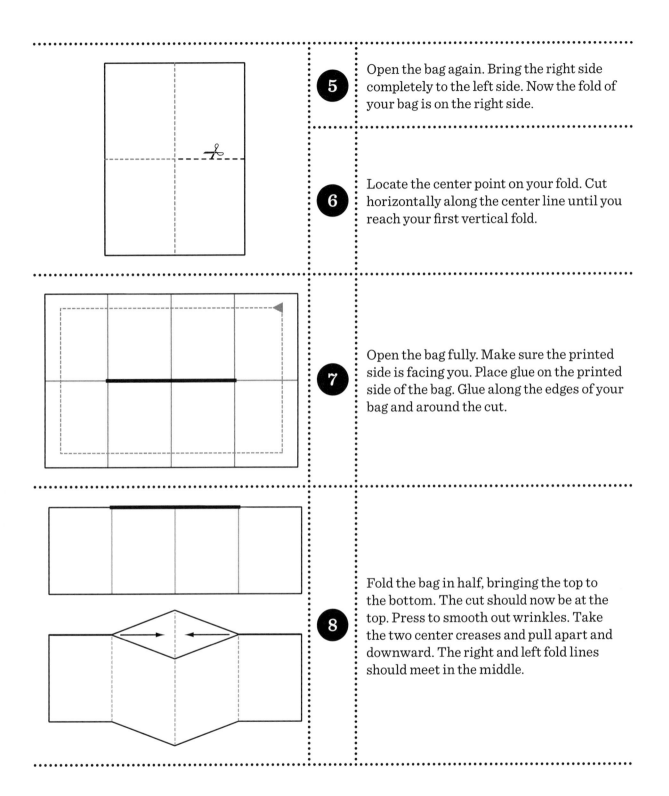

5 Open the bag again. Bring the right side completely to the left side. Now the fold of your bag is on the right side.

6 Locate the center point on your fold. Cut horizontally along the center line until you reach your first vertical fold.

7 Open the bag fully. Make sure the printed side is facing you. Place glue on the printed side of the bag. Glue along the edges of your bag and around the cut.

8 Fold the bag in half, bringing the top to the bottom. The cut should now be at the top. Press to smooth out wrinkles. Take the two center creases and pull apart and downward. The right and left fold lines should meet in the middle.

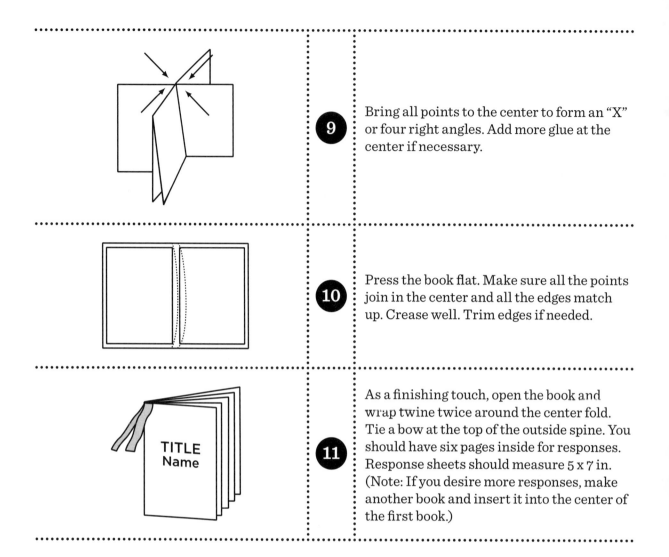

9 Bring all points to the center to form an "X" or four right angles. Add more glue at the center if necessary.

10 Press the book flat. Make sure all the points join in the center and all the edges match up. Crease well. Trim edges if needed.

11 As a finishing touch, open the book and wrap twine twice around the center fold. Tie a bow at the top of the outside spine. You should have six pages inside for responses. Response sheets should measure 5 x 7 in. (Note: If you desire more responses, make another book and insert it into the center of the first book.)

TITLE
Name

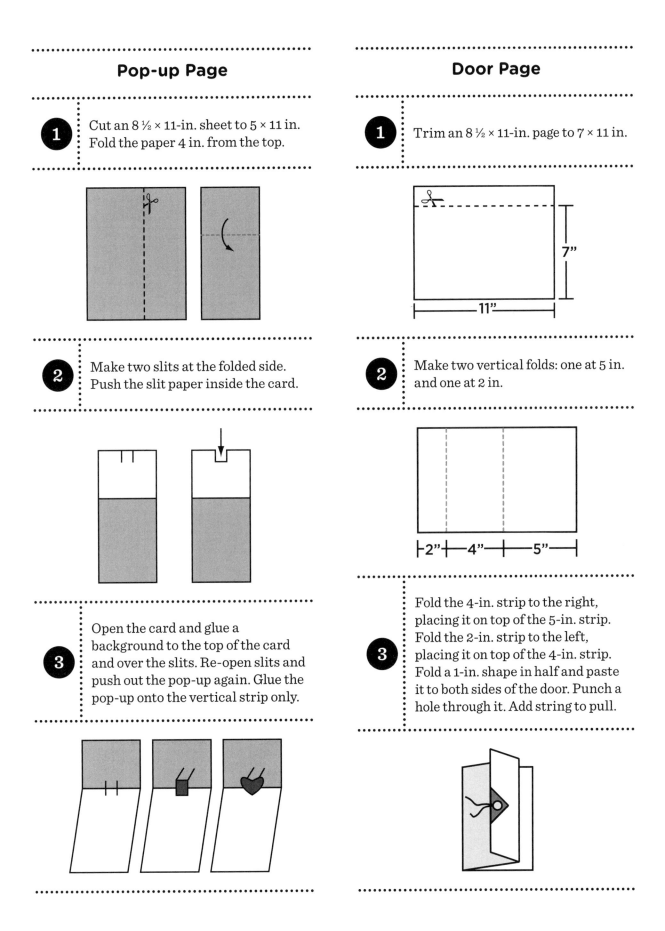

Pop-up Page

1 Cut an 8 ½ × 11-in. sheet to 5 × 11 in. Fold the paper 4 in. from the top.

2 Make two slits at the folded side. Push the slit paper inside the card.

3 Open the card and glue a background to the top of the card and over the slits. Re-open slits and push out the pop-up again. Glue the pop-up onto the vertical strip only.

Door Page

1 Trim an 8 ½ × 11-in. page to 7 × 11 in.

7"

11"

2 Make two vertical folds: one at 5 in. and one at 2 in.

2"—4"—5"

3 Fold the 4-in. strip to the right, placing it on top of the 5-in. strip. Fold the 2-in. strip to the left, placing it on top of the 4-in. strip. Fold a 1-in. shape in half and paste it to both sides of the door. Punch a hole through it. Add string to pull.

Basic Book Pocket Template

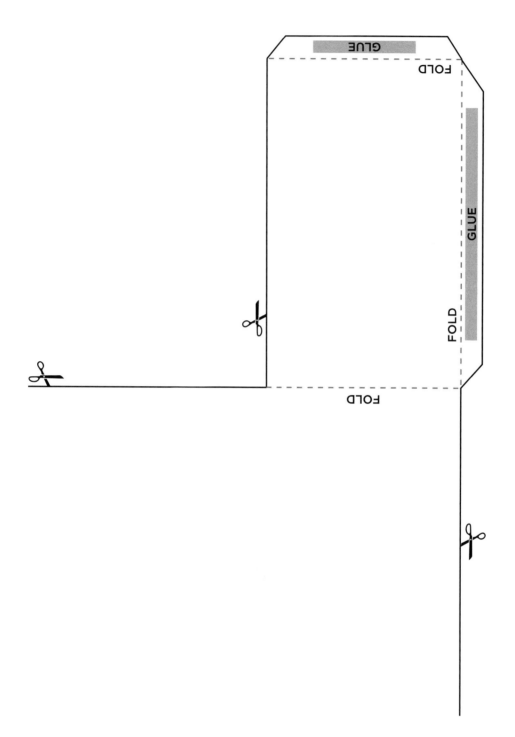

Basic Book Text Box Template

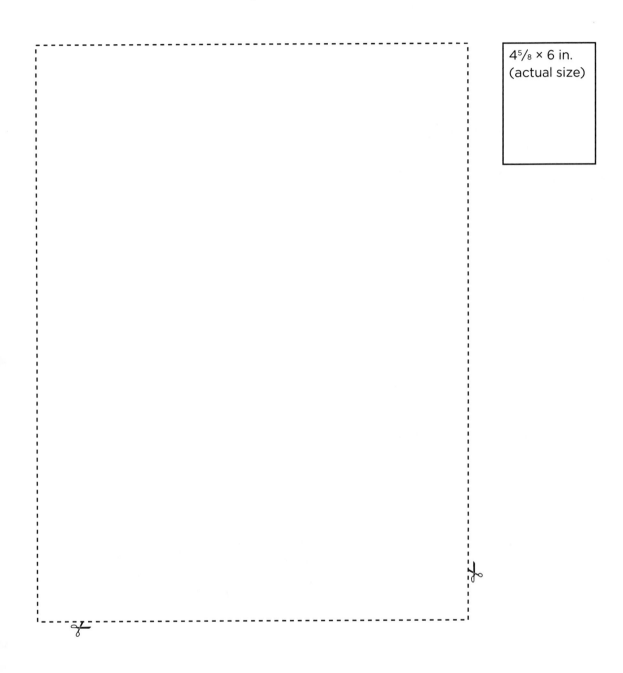

4⅝ × 6 in.
(actual size)

The Panel Book

Supplies

One grocery bag

Glue stick

White school glue

Scissors or paper cutter

One sheet of card stock cut to 7 × 11 in.

Six sheets of assorted colored card stock cut to 5 × 7 in.

1 yard of twine to tie book closed

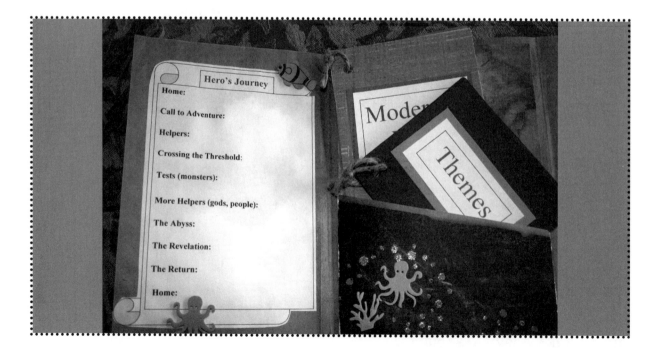

The Panel Book

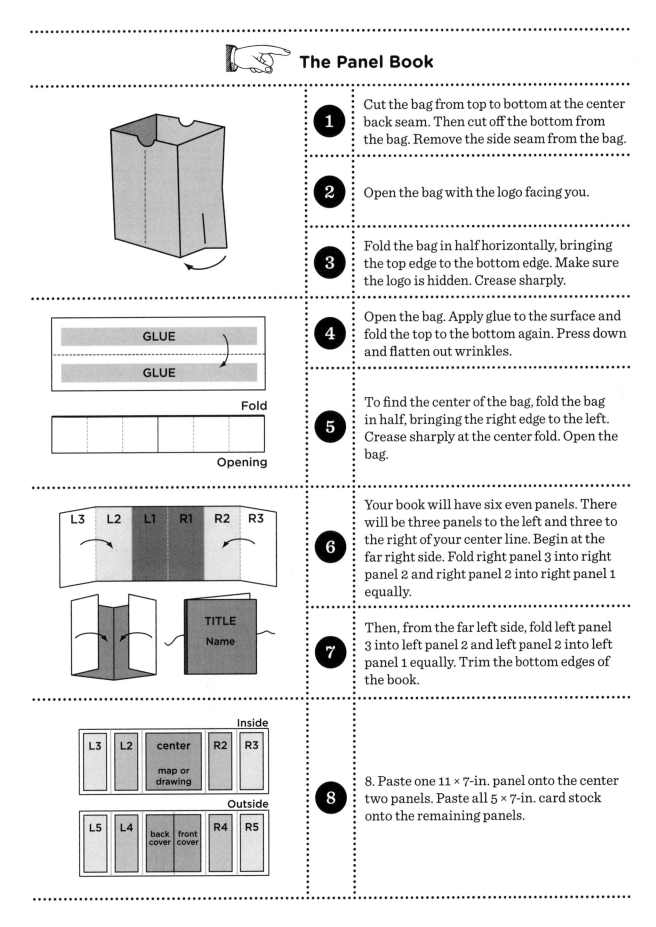

1 Cut the bag from top to bottom at the center back seam. Then cut off the bottom from the bag. Remove the side seam from the bag.

2 Open the bag with the logo facing you.

3 Fold the bag in half horizontally, bringing the top edge to the bottom edge. Make sure the logo is hidden. Crease sharply.

4 Open the bag. Apply glue to the surface and fold the top to the bottom again. Press down and flatten out wrinkles.

5 To find the center of the bag, fold the bag in half, bringing the right edge to the left. Crease sharply at the center fold. Open the bag.

6 Your book will have six even panels. There will be three panels to the left and three to the right of your center line. Begin at the far right side. Fold right panel 3 into right panel 2 and right panel 2 into right panel 1 equally.

7 Then, from the far left side, fold left panel 3 into left panel 2 and left panel 2 into left panel 1 equally. Trim the bottom edges of the book.

8 8. Paste one 11 × 7-in. panel onto the center two panels. Paste all 5 × 7-in. card stock onto the remaining panels.

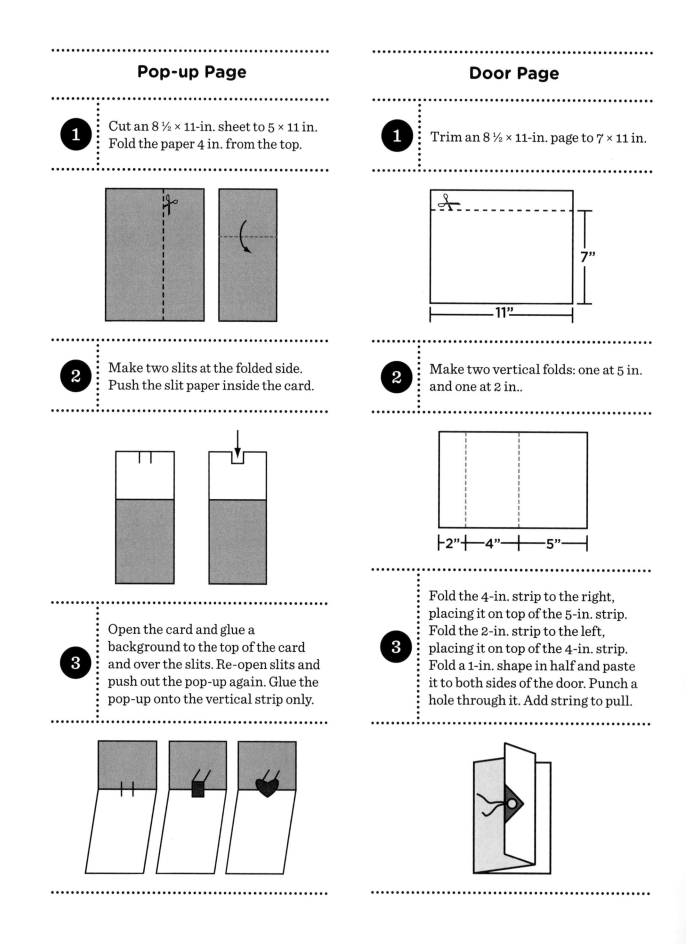

Pop-up Page

1 Cut an 8 ½ × 11-in. sheet to 5 × 11 in. Fold the paper 4 in. from the top.

2 Make two slits at the folded side. Push the slit paper inside the card.

3 Open the card and glue a background to the top of the card and over the slits. Re-open slits and push out the pop-up again. Glue the pop-up onto the vertical strip only.

Door Page

1 Trim an 8 ½ × 11-in. page to 7 × 11 in.

7"

11"

2 Make two vertical folds: one at 5 in. and one at 2 in..

2" 4" 5"

3 Fold the 4-in. strip to the right, placing it on top of the 5-in. strip. Fold the 2-in. strip to the left, placing it on top of the 4-in. strip. Fold a 1-in. shape in half and paste it to both sides of the door. Punch a hole through it. Add string to pull.

Panel Book Pocket Template

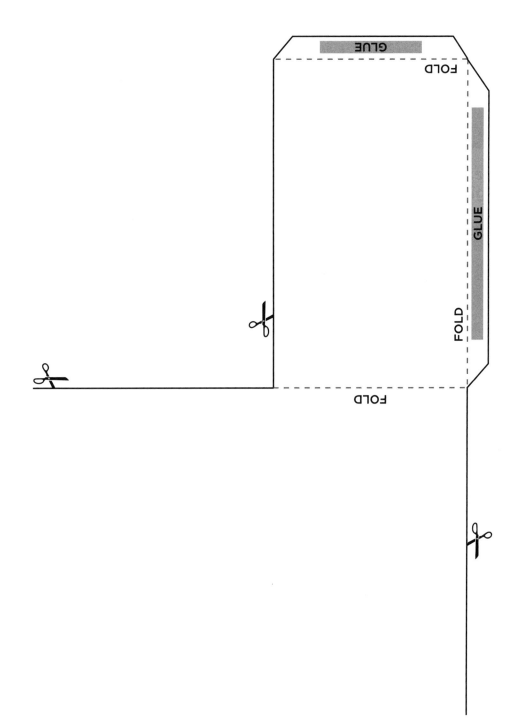

Panel Book Text Box Template

$4^{5}/_{8} \times 6$ in.
(actual size)

The Traveling Mat Book

Supplies

Six 8 ½ × 11-in. sheets of
65-lb. colored card stock

two sheets of color 1

two sheets of color 2

one sheet of color 3

one sheet of color 4

Ten sheets of colored computer
paper on which to place information

White school glue

Glue stick

Scissors or paper cutter

1 ft. of twine or ribbon

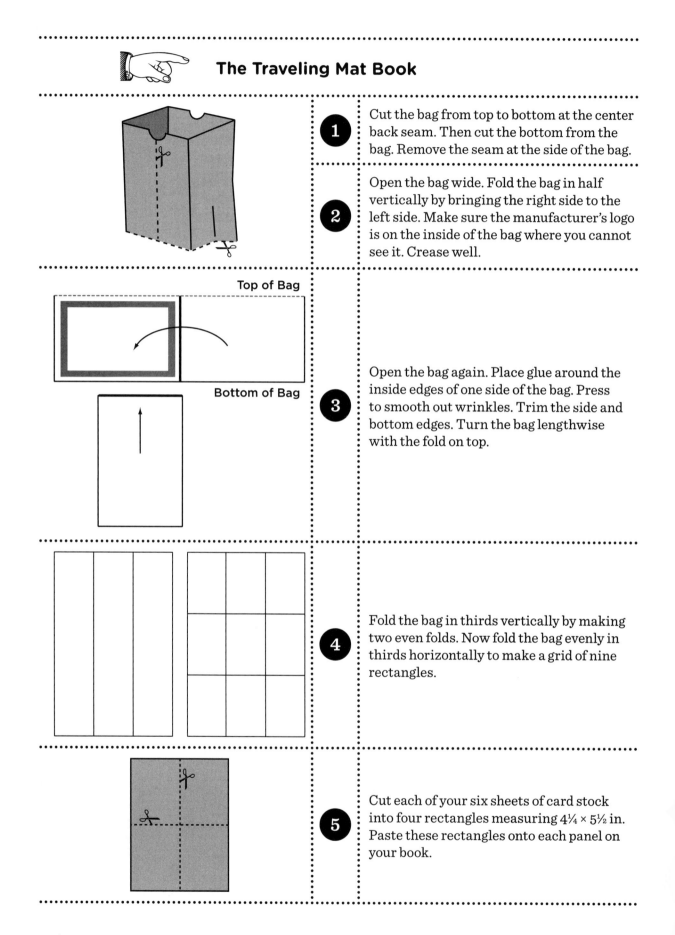

The Traveling Mat Book

1 Cut the bag from top to bottom at the center back seam. Then cut the bottom from the bag. Remove the seam at the side of the bag.

2 Open the bag wide. Fold the bag in half vertically by bringing the right side to the left side. Make sure the manufacturer's logo is on the inside of the bag where you cannot see it. Crease well.

Top of Bag

Bottom of Bag

3 Open the bag again. Place glue around the inside edges of one side of the bag. Press to smooth out wrinkles. Trim the side and bottom edges. Turn the bag lengthwise with the fold on top.

4 Fold the bag in thirds vertically by making two even folds. Now fold the bag evenly in thirds horizontally to make a grid of nine rectangles.

5 Cut each of your six sheets of card stock into four rectangles measuring 4¼ × 5½ in. Paste these rectangles onto each panel on your book.

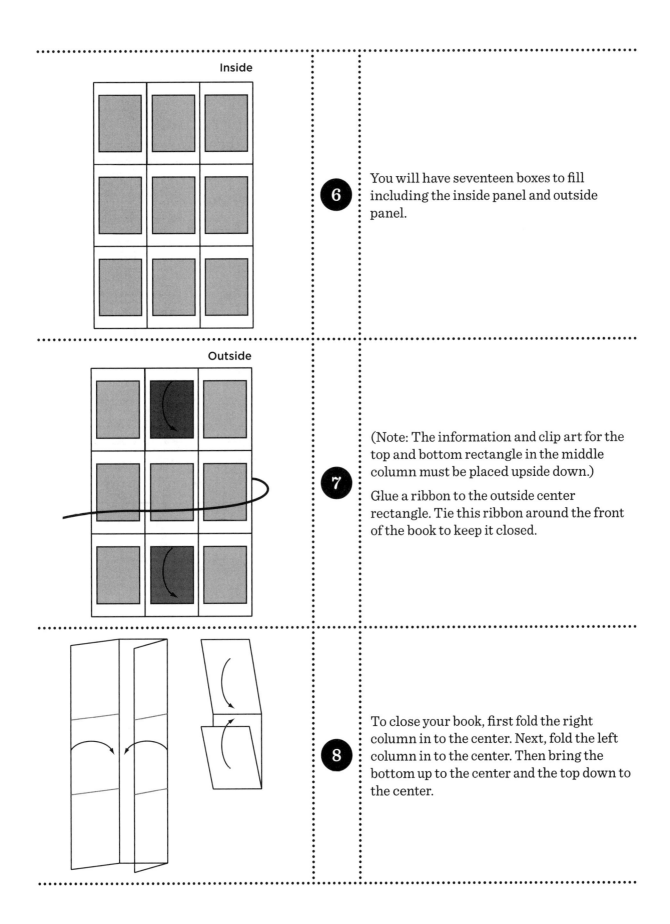

Inside

Outside

6 You will have seventeen boxes to fill including the inside panel and outside panel.

7 (Note: The information and clip art for the top and bottom rectangle in the middle column must be placed upside down.)

Glue a ribbon to the outside center rectangle. Tie this ribbon around the front of the book to keep it closed.

8 To close your book, first fold the right column in to the center. Next, fold the left column in to the center. Then bring the bottom up to the center and the top down to the center.

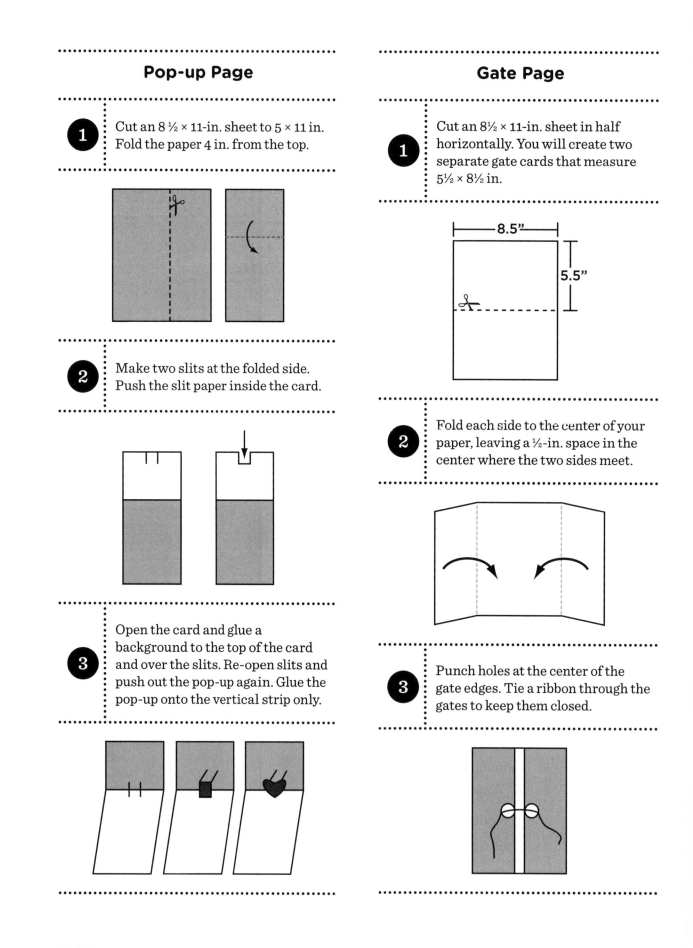

Pop-up Page

1 Cut an 8 ½ × 11-in. sheet to 5 × 11 in. Fold the paper 4 in. from the top.

2 Make two slits at the folded side. Push the slit paper inside the card.

3 Open the card and glue a background to the top of the card and over the slits. Re-open slits and push out the pop-up again. Glue the pop-up onto the vertical strip only.

Gate Page

1 Cut an 8½ × 11-in. sheet in half horizontally. You will create two separate gate cards that measure 5½ × 8½ in.

8.5"

5.5"

2 Fold each side to the center of your paper, leaving a ½-in. space in the center where the two sides meet.

3 Punch holes at the center of the gate edges. Tie a ribbon through the gates to keep them closed.

Traveling Mat Book Pocket Template

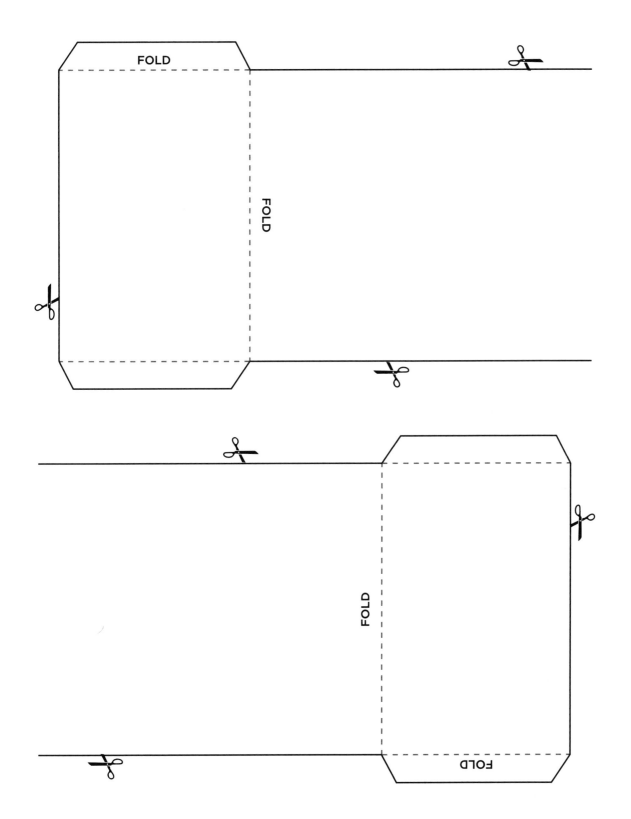

Traveling Mat Book Text Box Template

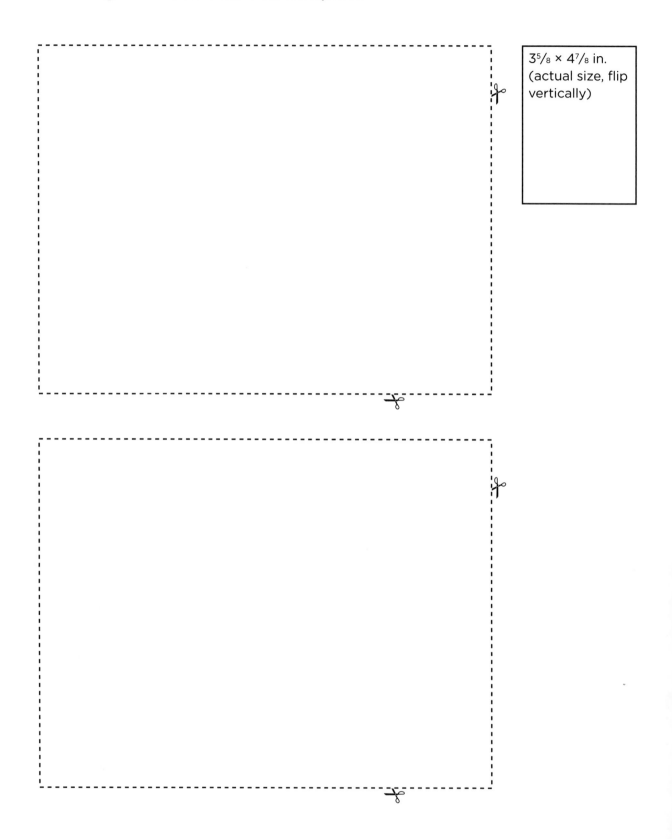

3⅝ × 4⅞ in. (actual size, flip vertically)

File Folder Books

The Flap Book

The Flap Book

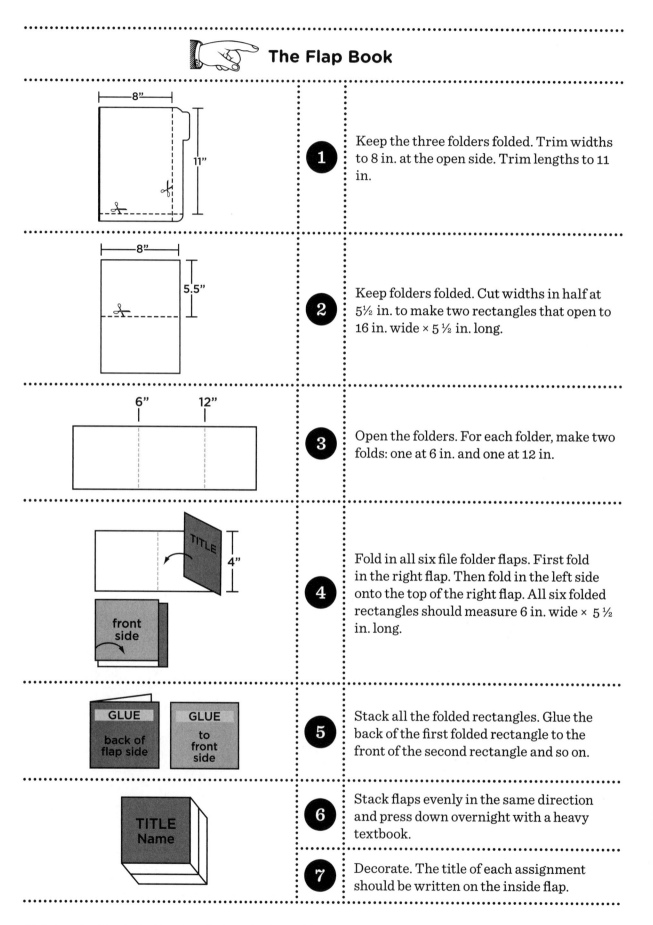

1 Keep the three folders folded. Trim widths to 8 in. at the open side. Trim lengths to 11 in.

2 Keep folders folded. Cut widths in half at 5½ in. to make two rectangles that open to 16 in. wide × 5 ½ in. long.

3 Open the folders. For each folder, make two folds: one at 6 in. and one at 12 in.

4 Fold in all six file folder flaps. First fold in the right flap. Then fold in the left side onto the top of the right flap. All six folded rectangles should measure 6 in. wide × 5 ½ in. long.

5 Stack all the folded rectangles. Glue the back of the first folded rectangle to the front of the second rectangle and so on.

6 Stack flaps evenly in the same direction and press down overnight with a heavy textbook.

7 Decorate. The title of each assignment should be written on the inside flap.

The Dutch Door Book

Supplies

Two file folders

Scissors or paper cutter

White glue stick

48 in. of twine or ribbon

Ten strips of 1 × 3-in. assorted colored paper on which to place information

The Dutch Door Book

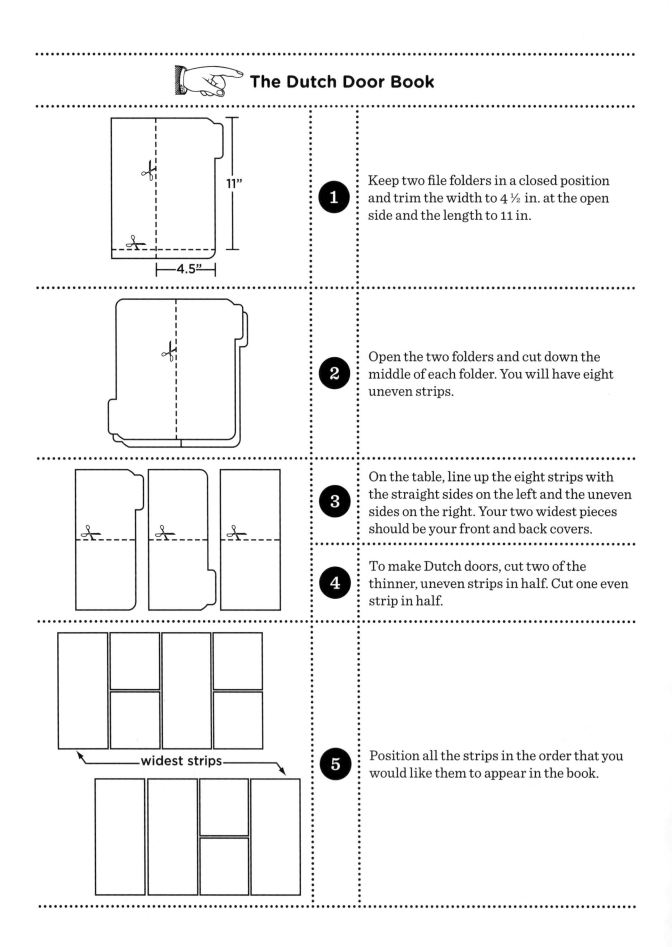

1 Keep two file folders in a closed position and trim the width to 4 ½ in. at the open side and the length to 11 in.

2 Open the two folders and cut down the middle of each folder. You will have eight uneven strips.

3 On the table, line up the eight strips with the straight sides on the left and the uneven sides on the right. Your two widest pieces should be your front and back covers.

4 To make Dutch doors, cut two of the thinner, uneven strips in half. Cut one even strip in half.

5 Position all the strips in the order that you would like them to appear in the book.

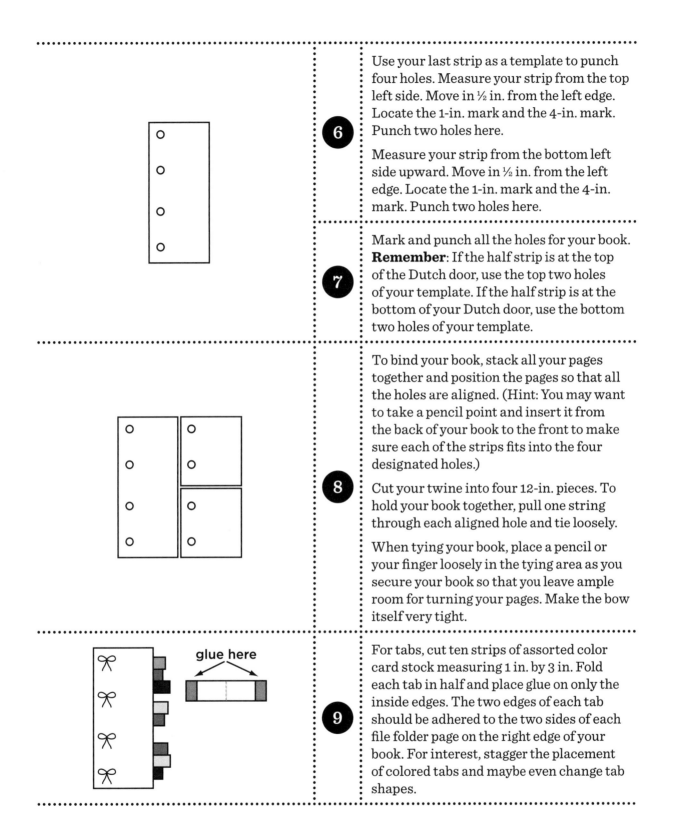

6 Use your last strip as a template to punch four holes. Measure your strip from the top left side. Move in ½ in. from the left edge. Locate the 1-in. mark and the 4-in. mark. Punch two holes here.

Measure your strip from the bottom left side upward. Move in ½ in. from the left edge. Locate the 1-in. mark and the 4-in. mark. Punch two holes here.

7 Mark and punch all the holes for your book. **Remember**: If the half strip is at the top of the Dutch door, use the top two holes of your template. If the half strip is at the bottom of your Dutch door, use the bottom two holes of your template.

8 To bind your book, stack all your pages together and position the pages so that all the holes are aligned. (Hint: You may want to take a pencil point and insert it from the back of your book to the front to make sure each of the strips fits into the four designated holes.)

Cut your twine into four 12-in. pieces. To hold your book together, pull one string through each aligned hole and tie loosely.

When tying your book, place a pencil or your finger loosely in the tying area as you secure your book so that you leave ample room for turning your pages. Make the bow itself very tight.

glue here

9 For tabs, cut ten strips of assorted color card stock measuring 1 in. by 3 in. Fold each tab in half and place glue on only the inside edges. The two edges of each tab should be adhered to the two sides of each file folder page on the right edge of your book. For interest, stagger the placement of colored tabs and maybe even change tab shapes.

Dutch Door Book Text Box Template

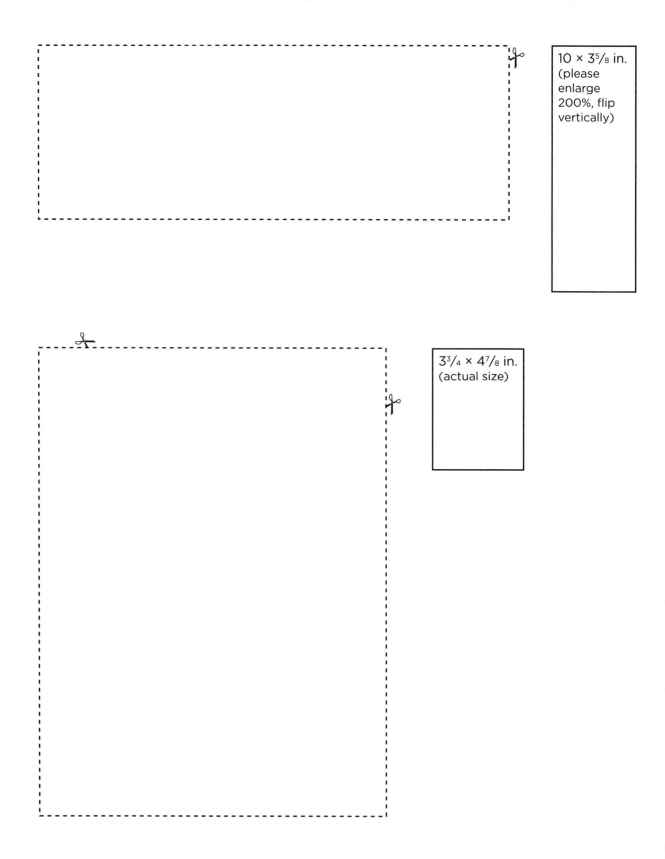

10 × 3⅝ in. (please enlarge 200%, flip vertically)

3¾ × 4⅞ in. (actual size)

The Expanding Book

Supplies

Three file folders

Six sheets plain or colored computer paper on which to place information

18 in. of ribbon or twine

White school glue

Glue stick for paper

Scissors or paper cutter

The Expanding Book

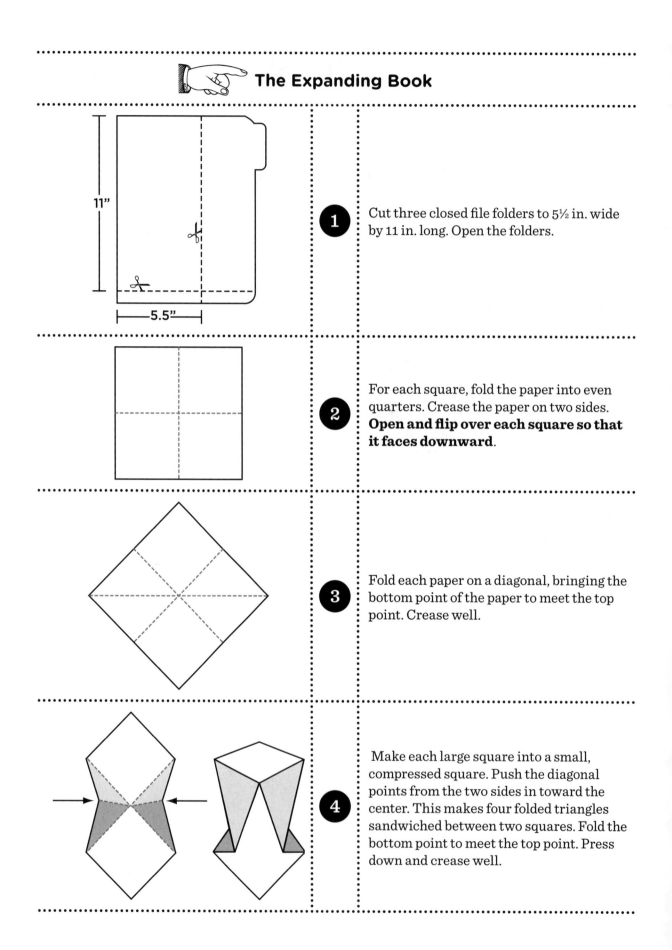

1 Cut three closed file folders to 5½ in. wide by 11 in. long. Open the folders.

2 For each square, fold the paper into even quarters. Crease the paper on two sides. **Open and flip over each square so that it faces downward.**

3 Fold each paper on a diagonal, bringing the bottom point of the paper to meet the top point. Crease well.

4 Make each large square into a small, compressed square. Push the diagonal points from the two sides in toward the center. This makes four folded triangles sandwiched between two squares. Fold the bottom point to meet the top point. Press down and crease well.

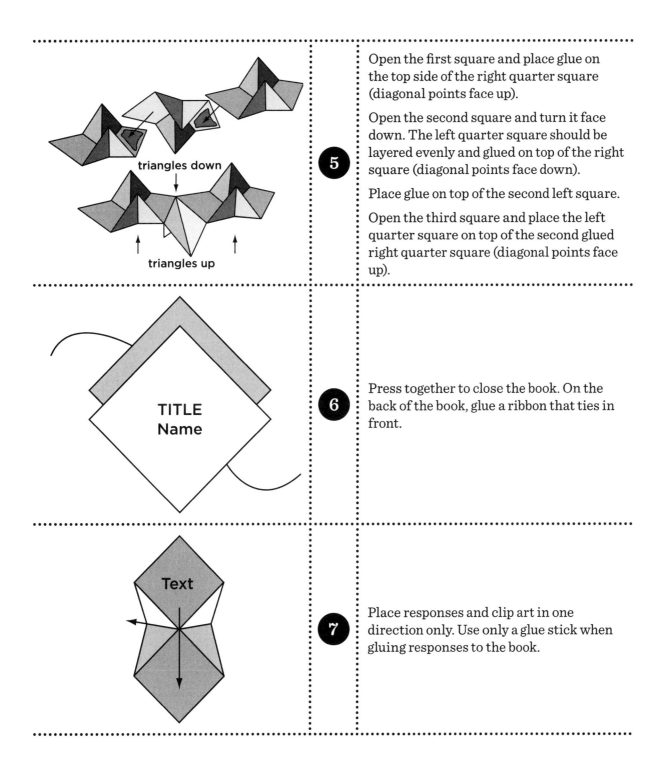

triangles down

triangles up

TITLE
Name

Text

5 Open the first square and place glue on the top side of the right quarter square (diagonal points face up).

Open the second square and turn it face down. The left quarter square should be layered evenly and glued on top of the right square (diagonal points face down).

Place glue on top of the second left square.

Open the third square and place the left quarter square on top of the second glued right quarter square (diagonal points face up).

6 Press together to close the book. On the back of the book, glue a ribbon that ties in front.

7 Place responses and clip art in one direction only. Use only a glue stick when gluing responses to the book.

Expanding Book Text Box Template

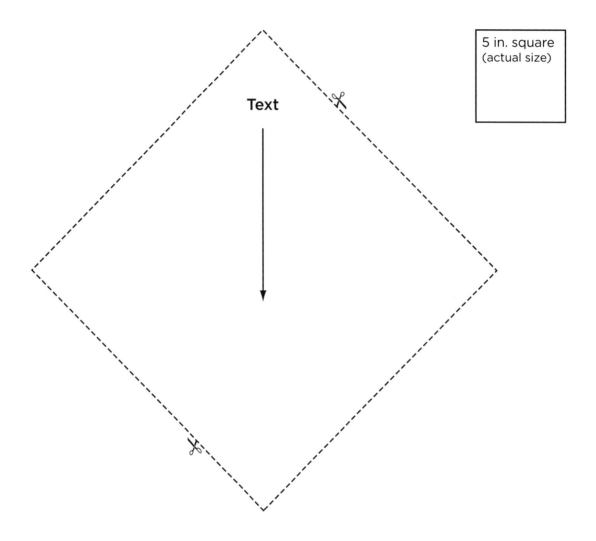

5 in. square
(actual size)

Text

Using a ruler and a colored marker, trace
the outline of your box. This adds a playful,
colorful touch.

Expanding Book Text Triangle Template

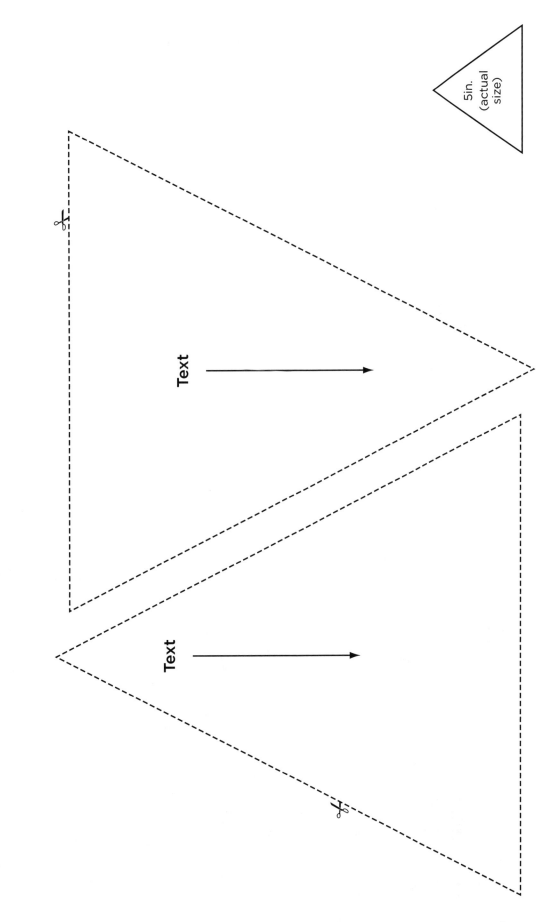

5in.
(actual
size)

Text →

Text →

The Never-ending Book

Supplies

Four sheets of assorted 8½ × 11-in. colored card stock

Four sheets plain or colored computer paper on which to place information

Scissors or paper cutter

Glue stick

Transparent tape

Hole punch

2 yards of twine

Decorative scissors

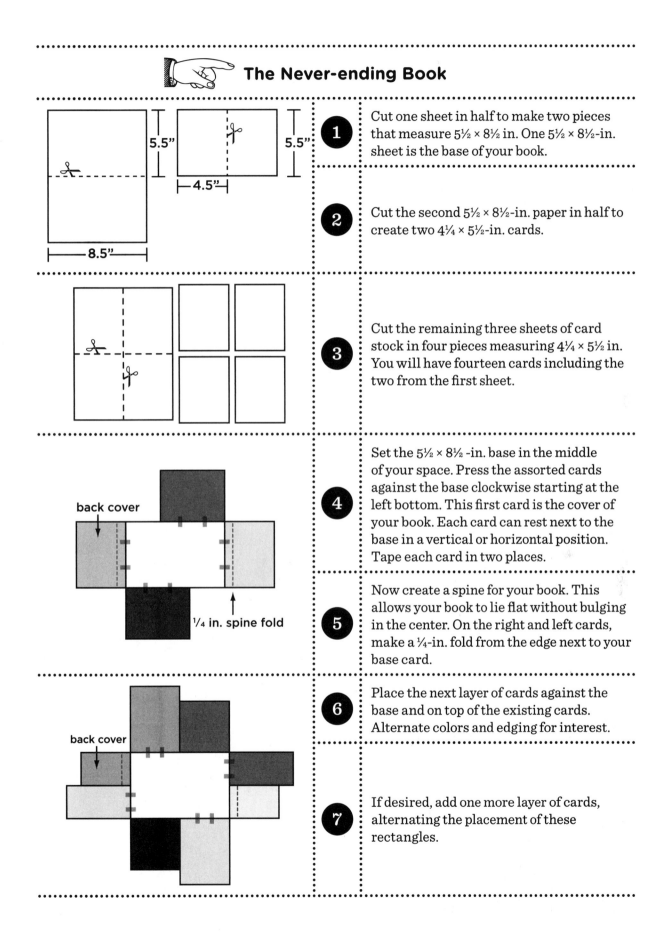

The Never-ending Book

1 Cut one sheet in half to make two pieces that measure 5½ × 8½ in. One 5½ × 8½-in. sheet is the base of your book.

2 Cut the second 5½ × 8½-in. paper in half to create two 4¼ × 5½-in. cards.

3 Cut the remaining three sheets of card stock in four pieces measuring 4¼ × 5½ in. You will have fourteen cards including the two from the first sheet.

4 Set the 5½ × 8½-in. base in the middle of your space. Press the assorted cards against the base clockwise starting at the left bottom. This first card is the cover of your book. Each card can rest next to the base in a vertical or horizontal position. Tape each card in two places.

5 Now create a spine for your book. This allows your book to lie flat without bulging in the center. On the right and left cards, make a ¼-in. fold from the edge next to your base card.

6 Place the next layer of cards against the base and on top of the existing cards. Alternate colors and edging for interest.

7 If desired, add one more layer of cards, alternating the placement of these rectangles.

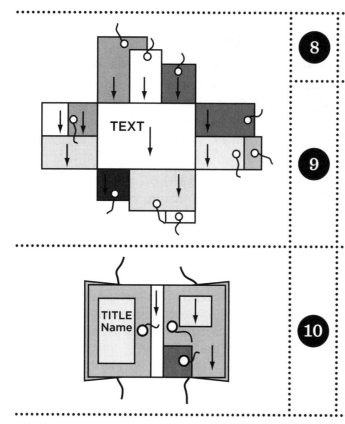

8 When the book is open, all responses should be in the same direction, moving from top to bottom.

9 Place a hole on the center edge of each card opposite the side that is taped. (This will let people know which way the doors open.) Thread a loop through each hole and pull the twine edges through the loop tightly.

10 When the book is closed, all pictures should be viewed in the same direction. Before decorating the front of the cards with drawings and clip art, close the book. Then, paste all artwork in the same direction, moving from top to bottom. The designs and titles can be oriented in either portrait or landscape mode.

Never-ending Book Text Box Template

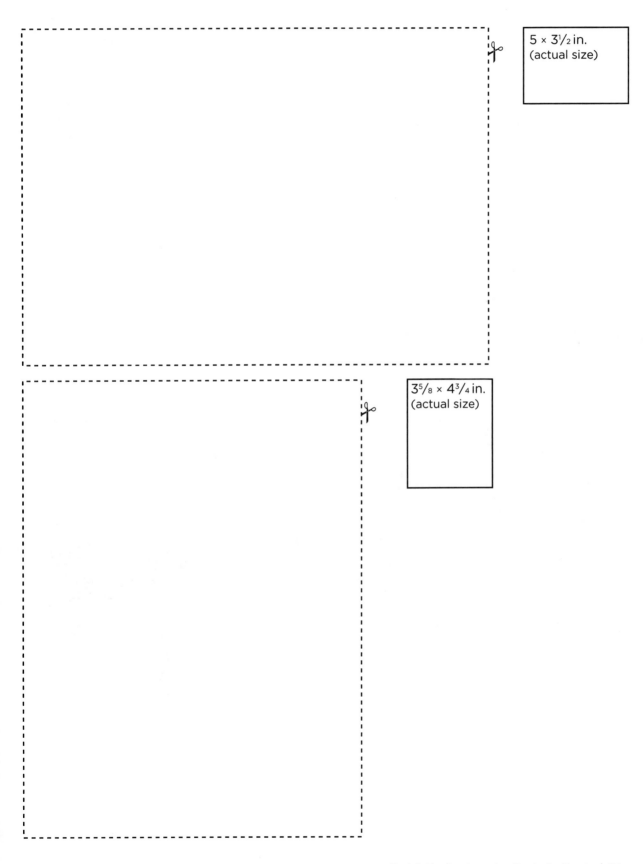

5 × 3½ in.
(actual size)

3⅝ × 4¾ in.
(actual size)

Paper Books

The Circle Book

Supplies

Four 12 × 12-in. sheets of card stock

Eight sheets plain or colored computer paper on which to place information

White school glue

Scissors

6-in. quarter-circle template

Hole punch

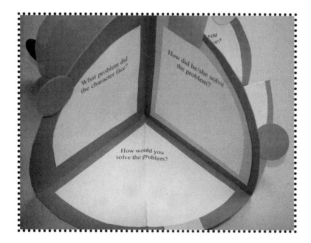

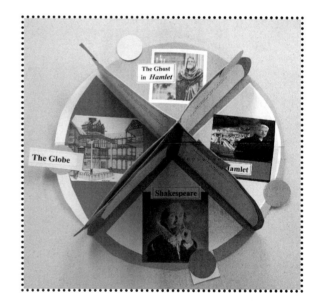

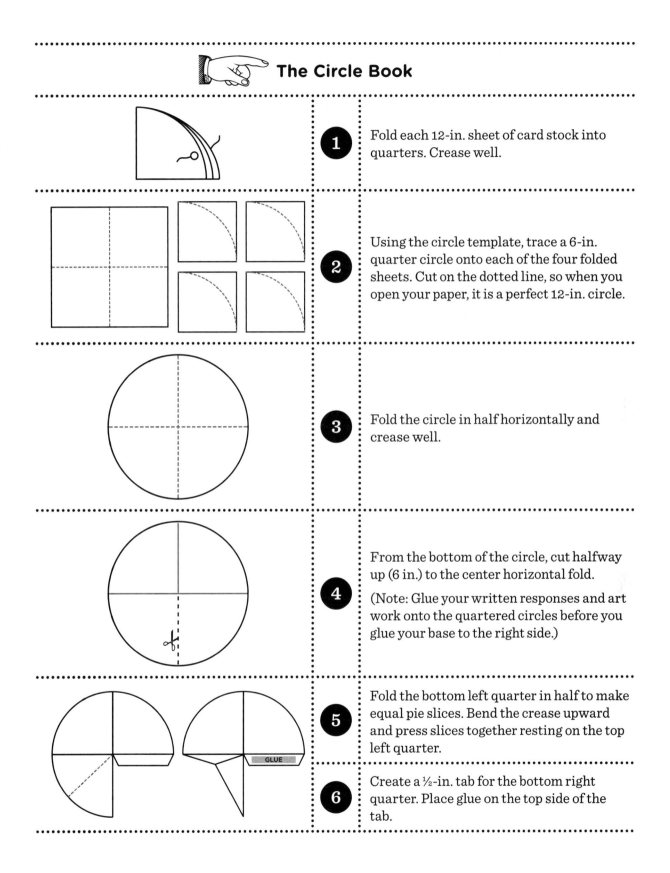

The Circle Book

1 Fold each 12-in. sheet of card stock into quarters. Crease well.

2 Using the circle template, trace a 6-in. quarter circle onto each of the four folded sheets. Cut on the dotted line, so when you open your paper, it is a perfect 12-in. circle.

3 Fold the circle in half horizontally and crease well.

4 From the bottom of the circle, cut halfway up (6 in.) to the center horizontal fold.

(Note: Glue your written responses and art work onto the quartered circles before you glue your base to the right side.)

5 Fold the bottom left quarter in half to make equal pie slices. Bend the crease upward and press slices together resting on the top left quarter.

6 Create a ½-in. tab for the bottom right quarter. Place glue on the top side of the tab.

GLUE

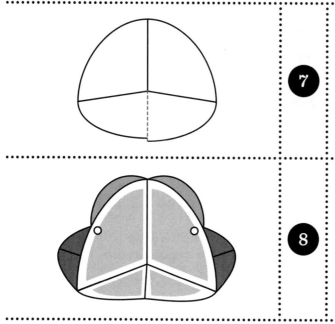

7 Bring the circle together by overlapping and adhering the bottom left section on top of the glued tab. Complete this for all four circles. Then, stack all four circles and glue them together: 1 onto 2, 2 onto 3, and 3 onto 4. Glue your written responses and art work onto the quartered circles before gluing your base to the right side.

8 Punch holes in the front and back panels about 2½ in. up from the bottom and ½ in. in from the edge. Add a ribbon to the cover and back to tie the book open or closed.

Circle Book Template

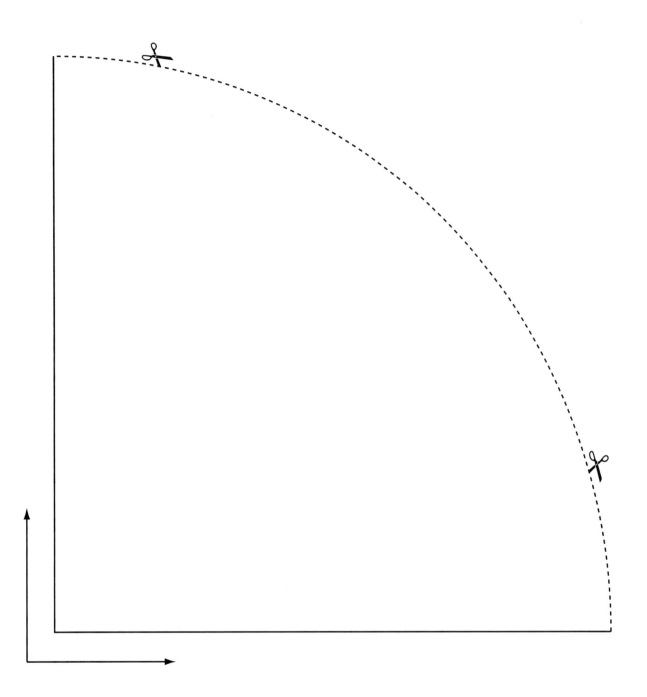

Fold each of your 12-in. sheets into four equal quarters.

For each folded paper, line up this right angle against your folds and **only cut along the dotted line**.

Circle Book Text Box Template

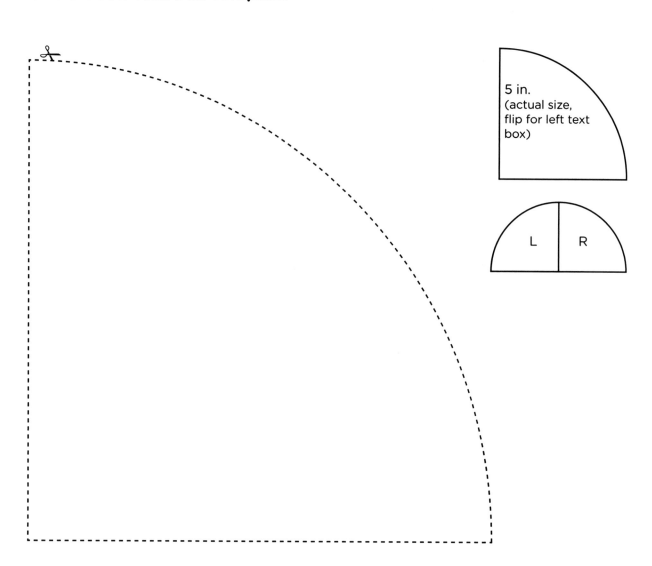

5 in.
(actual size,
flip for left text
box)

L | R

The Hanging Star Book

Supplies

Five 8 ½ × 8 ½ -in. sheets

White school glue

Glue stick

Scissors

2 ft. of ribbon or twine

Twenty-four 4-in. response squares

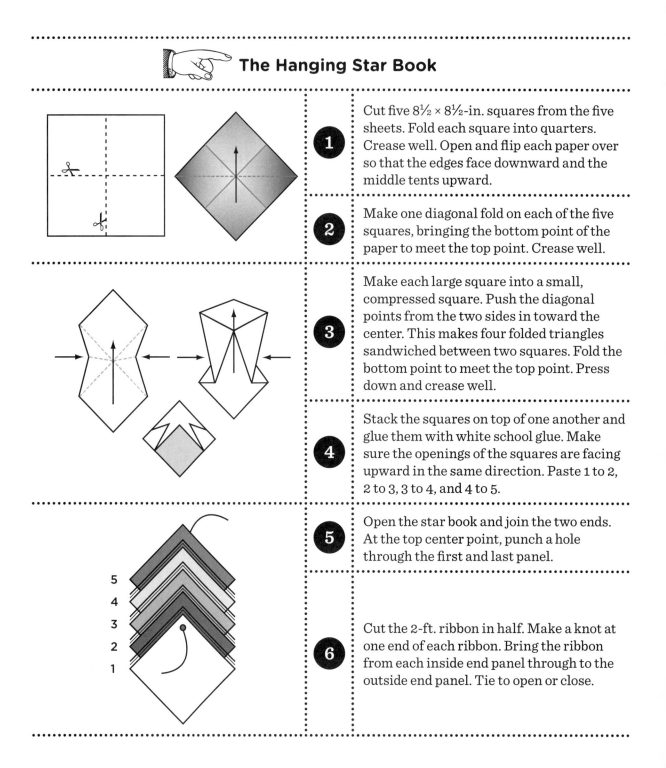

1. Cut five 8½ × 8½-in. squares from the five sheets. Fold each square into quarters. Crease well. Open and flip each paper over so that the edges face downward and the middle tents upward.

2. Make one diagonal fold on each of the five squares, bringing the bottom point of the paper to meet the top point. Crease well.

3. Make each large square into a small, compressed square. Push the diagonal points from the two sides in toward the center. This makes four folded triangles sandwiched between two squares. Fold the bottom point to meet the top point. Press down and crease well.

4. Stack the squares on top of one another and glue them with white school glue. Make sure the openings of the squares are facing upward in the same direction. Paste 1 to 2, 2 to 3, 3 to 4, and 4 to 5.

5. Open the star book and join the two ends. At the top center point, punch a hole through the first and last panel.

6. Cut the 2-ft. ribbon in half. Make a knot at one end of each ribbon. Bring the ribbon from each inside end panel through to the outside end panel. Tie to open or close.

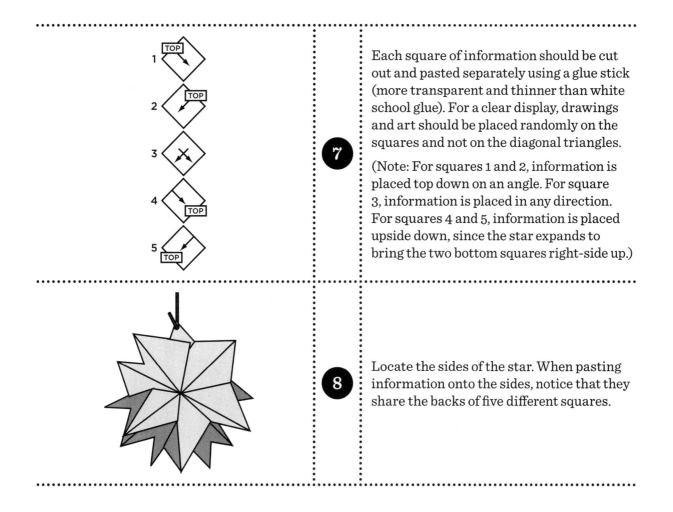

Each square of information should be cut out and pasted separately using a glue stick (more transparent and thinner than white school glue). For a clear display, drawings and art should be placed randomly on the squares and not on the diagonal triangles.

(Note: For squares 1 and 2, information is placed top down on an angle. For square 3, information is placed in any direction. For squares 4 and 5, information is placed upside down, since the star expands to bring the two bottom squares right-side up.)

Locate the sides of the star. When pasting information onto the sides, notice that they share the backs of five different squares.

Hanging Star Book Text Box Template

4 × 4 in.
(actual size)

Using a ruler and a colored marker, trace the outline of your triangle. This adds a playful, colorful touch.

PART 3

ASSESSING AMAZING HANDS-ON LITERATURE PROJECTS

Choosing Product-based Assessment

For almost a century, educators have emphasized the importance of hands-on, experiential learning. Many teachers believe that having students "do" creates significantly longer-lasting benefits than having them simply recall material for a test. These interactive projects engage and empower students, allowing them to create new material rather than mimic what they have just learned.

Product-based assessments encourage students to be self-directed individuals, problem solvers, effective communicators, and accountable, goal-oriented people.

At the outset, it is important for teachers to establish desired outcomes and then decide what route will be most effective for students to master these competencies. Using product-based assessments permits teachers to measure students' mastery of specific skills and competencies.

Each keepsake literature project requires students to complete multiple activities and products at the beginning, in the middle, and at the end of a unit. Then, as a culminating activity, students integrate all the assignments into a single compact book of everything central to the unit. By assigning many tasks within a unit, teachers give students the opportunity to demonstrate several proficiencies. These keepsakes require students to actively analyze, synthesize, and apply what they have learned in a substantial manner. Students profit from creating a project because they feel ownership of the work they actually do.

Creating a scoring guide is a great assessment tool. By providing the rubric at the start of the assignment, teachers make students aware of the project expectations. Teachers seek to evaluate students' performances based on the sum of a full range of criteria. Since there are numerous assignments, various skills will be targeted. Students know they will be evaluated on criteria such as sources, content, organization, writing conventions, appearance, and creativity.

Four Grading Divisions

Teachers have different grading formats and preferences, but the following pages offer four different rubrics to assess students' project competencies.

Amazing Literature Project Rubric A

NAME	

Circle all that apply to student's work.

SUPERIOR

1. All requirements are met and exceeded.

2. The information is gathered from a variety of quality electronic and print sources. It is cited and documented in the desired format.

3. The project is focused and purposeful, reflecting insight into all writing situations.

4. The development of the support is substantial, specific, relevant, and concrete. The student shows commitment to and involvement with the project and uses creative writing strategies.

5. The organizational pattern provides for a logical progression of ideas. Effective use of transitional devices contributes to a sense of completeness. There is a freshness of expression.

6. The sentence structure is varied, and few, if any, convention errors occur in mechanics, usage, punctuation, and spelling.

7. The project makes excellent use of design graphics, pictures, diagrams, and illustrations.

8. The project shows a large amount of creativity. Ideas are exceptional and inventive in their display. Much time and effort expended is highly evident in this project.

GOOD

1. All requirements are met.

2. The information is gathered from a variety of quality electronic and print sources. Most information is cited and documented in the desired format.

3. The content includes essential knowledge about topics. The support is developed through ample use of specific details and examples.

4. The writing is focused on the topic, and its organizational pattern provides for a logical progression of ideas. Effective use of transitional devices contributes to a sense of completeness. The writing demonstrates a mature command of language, and there is variation in sentence structure.

5. The writing generally follows the conventions of mechanics, usage, punctuation, and spelling. The writer makes one to two errors that distract the reader from the content.

6. The project makes good use of design graphics, pictures, diagrams, and illustrations.

7. The project shows creativity. Ideas are good and are displayed inventively. Time and effort spent on this project is evident.

FAIR

1. Requirements are not completely met.

2. The information is gathered from a limited range of sources. Minimal effort is evident in selecting quality sources. Not all information is documented in the desired format.

3. The content includes some essential information. The support is consistently developed, but it lacks specificity.

4. An organizational pattern is demonstrated, but the response lacks a logical progression of ideas. It contains loosely related ideas and few transitional devices. Word choice is adequate, and variation in sentence structure is only moderately demonstrated.

5. The writer makes several errors in following the conventions of mechanics, usage, punctuation, and spelling that distract the reader from the content.

6. The project makes insufficient use of design graphics, pictures, diagrams, and illustrations. This limits the reader's understanding of the topics.

7. The project shows little creativity. Ideas are typical and are displayed in an unenergetic way. A moderate amount of time and effort is evident in this project.

POOR OR MISSING

1. Many requirements are not met or are missing.

2. There is little or no source information. Documentation in the desired format is not present.

3. Content is minimal. The development of the support is erratic and nonspecific, and ideas are repeated or not present. Support consists of generalizations or fragmentary lists.

4. The writing addresses topics but loses focus by including extraneous or loosely related ideas. The response has an organizational pattern but lacks a sense of completeness or closure. Word choice is limited, predictable, vague, or obscure in meaning.

5. Frequent errors occur in the basic conventions of sentence structure, mechanics, usage, and punctuation. These mistakes distract the reader from understanding the content.

6. The project lacks the use of design graphics, pictures, diagrams, and illustrations. This hinders the reader's understanding of the topics.

7. The project shows no creativity. The ideas belong to other people, but the student does not give credit. It is not customized in an orderly way and appears random and confusing. Very little attention, if any, was expended on this project.

Amazing Literature Project Rubric B

NAME

PROJECT ASSESSMENT CRITERIA	SUPERIOR POINT VALUE ____	GOOD POINT VALUE ____	FAIR POINT VALUE ____	POOR POINT VALUE ____
Requirements	All requirements are met and exceeded.	All requirements are met.	Requirements are not completely met.	Many requirements are not met or are missing.
Sources	The information is gathered from a variety of quality electronic and print sources. It is cited and documented in a desired format.	The information is gathered from a variety of quality electronic and print sources. Most information is cited and documented in a desired format.	The information is gathered from a limited range of sources. Minimal effort is evident in selecting quality sources. Not all information is documented in a desired format.	There is little or no source information. Documentation in a desired format is not present.
Content	The project is focused and purposeful and reflects insight into all writing situations. Development of the support is substantial, specific, relevant, and concrete. The student shows commitment to and involvement with the project and may use creative writing strategies.	The content includes essential knowledge about topics. The support is developed through ample use of specific details and examples.	The content includes some essential information. Support is consistently developed, but it may lack specificity.	Content is minimal. The development of the support is erratic and nonspecific, and ideas are repeated or not present. Support consists of generalizations or fragmentary lists.
Organization	The organizational pattern provides for a logical progression of ideas. There is a freshness of expression. Effective use of transitional devices contributes to a sense of completeness.	The writing is focused on the topic, and its organizational pattern provides for a logical progression of ideas. Effective use of transitional devices contributes to a sense of completeness. The writing demonstrates a mature command of language, and there is variation in sentence structure.	An organizational pattern is demonstrated, but the response may lack a logical progression of ideas. It contains loosely related ideas and few transitional devices. Word choice is adequate, and variation in sentence structure is only moderately demonstrated.	The writing addresses topics but loses focus by including extraneous or loosely related ideas. The response has an organizational pattern, but it lacks a sense of completeness or closure. Word choice may be limited, predictable, vague, or obscure in meaning.
Conventions: Grammar, Usage, and Mechanics	The sentence structure is varied, and few, if any, convention errors occur in mechanics, usage, punctuation, and spelling.	The writing generally follows the conventions of mechanics, usage, punctuation, and spelling. The writer makes one or two errors that distract the reader from the content.	The writer makes several errors in following the conventions of mechanics, usage, punctuation, and spelling that distract the reader from the content.	Frequent errors occur in the basic conventions of sentence structure, mechanics, usage, and punctuation. These mistakes distract the reader from understanding the content.
Attractiveness	The project makes excellent use of design graphics, pictures, diagrams, and illustrations.	The project makes good use of design graphics, pictures, diagrams, and illustrations.	The project makes insufficient use of design graphics, pictures, diagrams, and illustrations. This limits the reader's understanding of the topics.	The project lacks the use of design graphics, pictures, diagrams, and illustrations. This hinders the reader's understanding of the topics.
Creativity	The project shows a large amount of creativity. Ideas are exceptional and inventive in their display. Much time and effort expended is highly evident in this project.	The project shows creativity. Ideas are good and are displayed inventively. Time and effort spent on this project are evident.	The project shows little creativity. Ideas are typical and are displayed in an unenergetic way. A moderate amount of time and effort is evident in this project.	The project shows no creativity. The ideas belong to other people, but the student does not give credit. It is not customized in an orderly way and appears random and confusing. Very little attention, if any, was expended in this project.

Amazing Literature Project Rubric C

NAME		DATE	
TEACHER		CLASS	

POINTS EARNED/ TOTAL POSSIBLE POINTS

1. The project requirements are met. There are no missing assignments.

    SUPERIOR   GOOD   FAIR   POOR/MISSING   _____

2. The project uses primary and secondary sources, which include information and quotes that are credible and cited correctly.

    SUPERIOR   GOOD   FAIR   POOR/MISSING   _____

3. The project content relates to the main topics and includes several supporting details and/or examples.

    SUPERIOR   GOOD   FAIR   POOR/MISSING   _____

4. The project organization is logical and coherent.

    SUPERIOR   GOOD   FAIR   POOR/MISSING   _____

5. The project responses use correct grammar, usage, and mechanics.

    SUPERIOR   GOOD   FAIR   POOR/MISSING   _____

6. The project uses clear and attractive design graphics, pictures, diagrams, and illustrations.

    SUPERIOR   GOOD   FAIR   POOR/MISSING   _____

7. The project shows a large amount of creativity. Ideas are original and inventive. Much effort went into planning and making the project.

    SUPERIOR   GOOD   FAIR   POOR/MISSING   _____

OVERALL GRADE:

COMMENTS

Amazing Literature Project Rubric D

NAME		DATE	
TEACHER		CLASS	

ASSIGNMENTS FOR THE AMAZING LITERATURE PROJECT	POINTS EARNED/ TOTAL POSSIBLE POINTS	SUPERIOR	GOOD	FAIR	POOR
1.					
2.					
3.					
4.					
5.					
6.					
7.					
8.					

OVERALL GRADE:

COMMENTS

Sample Projects and Worksheets
Travel Journal

NAME	
PASSPORT TO	

You have taken a wonderful journey into a great book. There were many notable landmarks of ideas for you to remember and many experiences from which you learned. Share your expedition by completing this travel journal. (This activity pairs well with the Dutch door book. See p. 61)

1. DESTINATION TO . . .	Describe the location and time period. Give geographical and historical background.
2. MAP	Print or create a map of this place.
3. THE PEOPLE I'VE MET	Give a physical description, personality description, and any significant background information on three people you've met.
4. SNAPSHOTS I'VE TAKEN	Take three pictures of any people, places, things, or events where you were. Explain their significance.
5. TRIP HIGHLIGHTS	Record six major events in chronological order.
6. REMEMBER THIS	Who said what and why?
7. UNEXPECTED MOMENT	Explain the unexpected event that occurred and how the person involved responded.
8. DANGEROUS WATERS AHEAD	Were there hints that a problem was brewing? Explain how this problem could or could not have been prevented.
9. SOUVENIRS AND MEMENTOS	List three important souvenirs or mementos you've collected from your trip. Explain their significance.
10. TOP FIVE THINGS I'VE LEARNED	Make a list of five important lessons about people or life that you learned from your journey.
11. I DON'T THINK I'M IN MY TOWN	Compare and contrast your world to the place you have traveled. Are there similarities? Differences?
12. I WISH THAT . . .	Describe something you wish had happened differently on your trip. What could have made the journey better?
13. GREETINGS FROM . . .	Now that your trip is over, create a postcard to send to the author about your overall feeling of this trip.
14. MY HOMETOWN	Pretend a character has come to visit you in your hometown. What clothes, books, movies, and activities would that character like and why?
15. TRAVEL AD	Design a travel advertisement for the trip's setting. Persuade people to travel to this destination. Include a drawing and a catchy phrase.
16. MAKING IT BIG	You're grown up and returning to this destination. You want to start a successful business. Describe the type of business you would start and why it would be so successful.

The Odyssey Project

NAME	
PROJECT DUE	

Materials Needed to Make Panel Book

– one large brown grocery bag   – ten sheets of assorted color card stock

– white school glue and glue sticks   – embellishments of choice

Following your teacher's instructions, create a handmade book of your responses to the epic poem, *The Odyssey*. Complete the following response assignments in a thorough, clear, and creative way. Use the templates provided by your teacher to help you.

---

1. MAP AND SHIP JOURNALS   _____ POINTS

On a map, highlight Odysseus's journey from Troy to home. Complete a Ship Journal for each island Odysseus visits.

Draw arrows designating the direction he sails, and chronologically number each place he travels. Color in the map artistically.

1. Troy
2. Land of the Lotus Eaters
3. Cyclopes
4. Aeolus (Wind God)
5. Aeaea (Circe)
6. Hades (Land of the Dead)
7. Sirens' Island
8. Scylla and Charybdis
9. Thrinacia (Helios—Sun God)
10. Ogygia (Calypso)
11. Phaeacia (King Antinous)
12. Ithica

---

2. ANCIENT GREEK BOOKMARKS   _____ POINTS

Choose twelve topics on Ancient Greece from the Internet to create twelve bookmarks.

For each bookmark, include the topic, a photo/drawing, and information.

Make each colorful, vibrant, and informative.

Mount each on colored card stock.

---

3. TERMS   _____ POINTS

Define the following terms creatively:

epic	epic hero	epic simile
epithet	in medias res	irony (dramatic and verbal)
omen	symbol	

---

4. MYTHICAL GOD OR MYTHICAL MONSTER POSTER   _____ POINTS

Include a name, drawing, and paragraph about your creature.

Your paragraph should include the location, occupation, purpose, good human qualities, and negative human qualities of your figure.

Reduce your original poster to fit on a 5 in.-wide × 7 in.-long piece of paper, and mount it on colored card stock.

5. EPIC HERO   _____ POINTS

Epic heroes possess superior human qualities. Explain how Odysseus fits each of the criterion for an epic hero.

6. HERO'S JOURNEY   _____ POINTS

Odysseus goes from the known world into an unknown world, then back to the known world.

7. THEMES   _____ POINTS

Discuss how each theme or central idea relates to *The Odyssey*.

1. A boy must struggle to become a man.
2. A soldier must struggle to return home after a war.
3. A king must struggle to regain his kingdom.
4. A person must face the challenges in life.
5. A person must use advice that is given.
6. Men cause their own destruction.

8. QUOTABLE QUOTES   _____ POINTS

Explain how each statement relates to the *The Odyssey*. Make sure you give a specific example to support your claim.

1. All's fair in love and war.
2. There's no place like home.
3. Beware of Greeks bearing gifts.
4. What goes around comes around.
5. Sometimes a little deceit is necessary.
6. The end justifies the means.
7. You shouldn't indulge freeloaders.
8. I'd rather be a live coward than a dead hero.

9. RELEVANCE IN THE MODERN WORLD   _____ POINTS

The Odyssey was written in 800 B.C., yet it is still relevant today.

1. Compare and contrast ancient Greece with the modern world.
2. Write a tabloid news article reporting the death of Antinous.
3. Create bumper-sticker slogans for each character listed.
4. Locate modern heroes in movies.
5. When soldiers return home from war, they experience difficulty. How are their experiences similar to Odysseus's?

10. PARK DESIGNER   _____ POINTS

On a 5-in. × 7-in. piece of paper, design an advertisement for an attraction at the new Odyssey Theme Park by Disney. Choose an event from the story on which to base your attraction. Your advertisement should name the attraction, include a drawing, and give a brief description highlighting the special features. You can select a land ride, a water ride, a store, or a restaurant. Remember, no violence please.

The Odyssey Ship Journal

Diary Entry #_____   Reported by _____

Location: **Weather:**

Why this destination?

Odysseus encounters antagonist:

Unique features:

Physical ability:

Intellectual prowess:

Good human qualities:

How does Odysseus deal with antagonist?

Consequence(s) of the encounter for Odysseus and his men

What does this antagonist represent or symbolize?

Drawing of the Encounter:

Temptations(s)/danger(s)/threat(s) posed to Odysseus and his men:

Of Mice and Men Project

NAME	
GRADE	/_____ POINTS

Remarks: **Excellent**   **Good**   **Fair**   **Missing**

ASSIGNMENTS	QUALITY OF WRITTEN RESPONSE	QUALITY OF VISUAL LAYOUT	QUALITY OF LEAD-IN, QUOTE, AND CITATION	POINTS
Cover: Title and Your Name				/___
1. The Author: John Steinbeck (Research)				/___
2. The Great Depression (Research)				/___
3. Migrant Farm Workers during the 1930s (Research)				/___
4. Lyrical and Naturalistic Writing				/___
5. Poverty				/___
6. The Unattainable American Dream for Candy				/___
7. Importance of Setting				/___
8. Significance of the Title				/___
9. Discrimination				/___
10. Role of Friendship				/___
11. Atmosphere of Doom				/___
12. Symbols				/___
13. The Shooting of Lennie				/___
14. The Price of a Farm Today				/___

1. The Author: John Steinbeck

Write two paragraphs about the author. Follow the outline below:

In paragraph one, describe the person

a. the man
b. his life
c. the time period in which he lived

In paragraph two, describe John Steinbeck as a writer. Consider topics and themes he chose to write about.

2. The Great Depression

The Great Depression began in the fall of 1929. It greatly affected all walks of life during that time period in America. On a separate piece of paper, draw and complete the following chart.

CAUSES OF THE GREAT DEPRESSION	EFFECTS OF THE GREAT DEPRESSION
1.	1.
2.	2.
3.	3.

3. Migrant Farm Workers during the 1930s

a. From which states was there a mass exodus and why did people leave?
b. How did the Californians treat the "Okies" and Mexicans when they arrived?
c. What difficulties did these migrant workers encounter?

4. Lyrical and Naturalistic Writing

In *Of Mice and Men*, John Steinbeck employs two styles of writing: lyrical and naturalistic. Think about the contrast between these two types. The author alternates between them to create certain effects. Write two paragraphs: The first paragraph should relate to Steinbeck's use of lyrical writing, and the second paragraph should relate to his use of naturalistic writing.

Lyrical writing is poetic and flowery. It uses sound devices, imagery, and figurative language to convey moods or ideas.

Naturalistic writing is down-to-earth, ungrammatical, and realistic. It captures the slang and colloquialisms of people of a certain time and at a certain place.

a. When does Steinbeck use **lyrical writing** (poetic language)?
b. Give two specific examples from the text.
c. By using this writing, what **message** is being conveyed?
d. When does Steinbeck use **naturalistic writing** (rough language)?
e. Give two specific examples from the text.
f. By using this naturalistic writing, what **contrast** is being set up by the author?

5. Poverty in *Of Mice and Men*

Two characters in the novel, George and Lennie, are among those migrant farm workers who have lived from one seasonal farming job to the next. They are poor and lonely, having very little except their dreams, each other, and hope for a better future. From your reading, create a chart on a separate piece of paper, such as the following, and give specific examples of how these conditions are portrayed in the novel, *Of Mice and Men*.

PHYSICAL CONDITIONS OF POVERTY	SPECIFIC EXAMPLE FROM THE TEXT
Poor living quarters	
Lack of luxuries	
Poor work environment	
EMOTIONAL CONDITIONS OF POVERTY	SPECIFIC EXAMPLE FROM TEXT
Financial dependence	
Abuse	
No control over one's destiny	

6. The Unattainable American Dream

Of Mice and Men takes place at a California ranch during the Depression. The characters are uneducated, lower-class people who are trying, with little success, to change their lives.

Candy was struggling with wanting more from life.

a. What was his present situation like?
b. Describe his search for the American Dream. Explain using a direct quote and specific examples from the text.
c. Why was he unable to obtain his dream?

7. Importance of Setting

The setting in the novel takes place over the course of four days. There are six different scenes, each beginning with a description of the setting. The following is a chart of the settings in the novel. Recreate this chart on a separate piece of paper, and list at least three significant events that occurred in each place.

SETTING	THREE IMPORTANT EVENTS FOR EACH SETTING
The clearing by the pool, about a quarter mile from the ranch, Thursday evening	
The bunkhouse of the ranch, Friday morning	
The bunkhouse, Friday evening	
The harness room in the barn, Saturday evening	
The barn Sunday afternoon	
The clearing by the pool, about a quarter mile from the ranch, Sunday evening	

8. Significance of the Title

The title of the novel, *Of Mice and Men*, is an allusion (reference) to a poem by the Scottish writer Robert Burns.

> *The best-laid schemes o' mice an' men*
> *Gang aft a-gley.*

This line, usually quoted as "The best laid plans of mice and men often go astray," illustrates the novel's main idea: Two major characters have plans that get crushed.

Write a paragraph answering the following questions. Be sure to use evidence from the text to support your opinions.

a. How is this an appropriate title for the book?
b. What plans do Lennie and George make?
c. How do their plans go astray?

9. Discrimination in *Of Mice and Men*

Discrimination is the act of seeing differences unfairly. Using the Anti-Defamation League's Pyramid of Hate, locate instances of discrimination in the novel. Write two paragraphs.

In paragraph one

a. Discuss how the ranchers discriminate against **Crooks** based on race.
b. Give one direct quote from the novel.
c. Place your opinion in the concluding statement.

In paragraph two

a. Discuss how the ranchers discriminate against **Curley's wife** because she is a woman.
b. Give one direct quote from the novel.
c. Place your opinion in the concluding statement.

The Anti-Defamation League's Pyramid of Hate

Discrimination is making a distinction in favor of or against a person or thing based on the group, class, or category to which a person or thing belongs rather than on individual merit.

In works of literature, many characters experience discrimination based on race, religion, gender, economics, and age, as well as many other aspects of society. The Anti-Defamation League has developed this Pyramid of Hate to educate people of the categories of hate and the hateful behaviors people exhibit that fall into specific categories. The League hopes that people will recognize discrimination at its smallest levels to prevent acts of hate from occurring.

The Anti-Defamation League's Pyramid of Hate

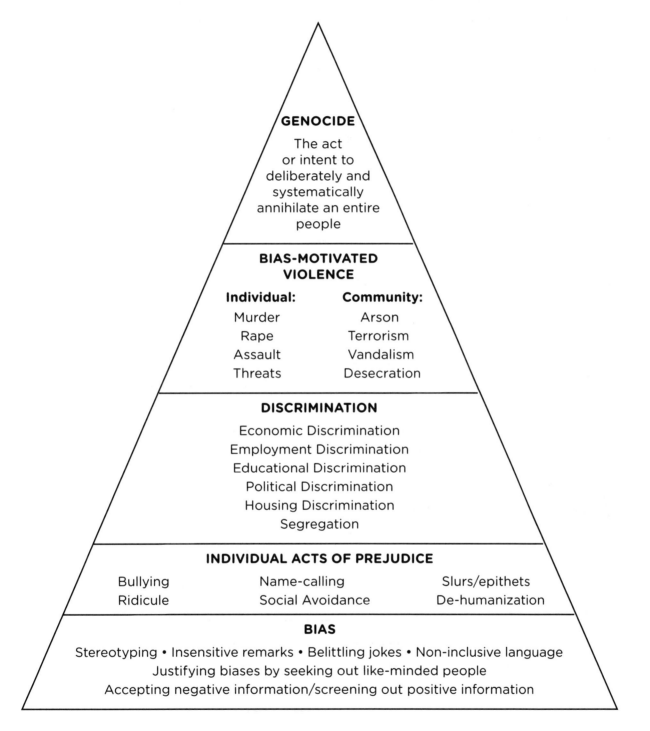

GENOCIDE
The act or intent to deliberately and systematically annihilate an entire people

BIAS-MOTIVATED VIOLENCE

Individual:
Murder
Rape
Assault
Threats

Community:
Arson
Terrorism
Vandalism
Desecration

DISCRIMINATION
Economic Discrimination
Employment Discrimination
Educational Discrimination
Political Discrimination
Housing Discrimination
Segregation

INDIVIDUAL ACTS OF PREJUDICE

Bullying
Ridicule

Name-calling
Social Avoidance

Slurs/epithets
De-humanization

BIAS
Stereotyping • Insensitive remarks • Belittling jokes • Non-inclusive language
Justifying biases by seeking out like-minded people
Accepting negative information/screening out positive information

10. Role of Friendship

George and Lennie travel together, unlike the other ranch hands. These men exhibit qualities important to a friendship. On a separate piece of paper, draw the following chart and explain how each of the following qualities is evident in the relationship of Lennie and George.

IMPORTANT QUALITIES IN A FRIENDSHIP	EXAMPLE OF EACH IN GEORGE AND LENNIE'S RELATIONSHIP
Loyalty	
Compassion (sensitivity to another person)	
Respect	
Honesty	
Trust	

11. Atmosphere of Doom in *Of Mice and Men*

John Steinbeck was a master at creating suspense. By letting us know little by little about Lennie's problem, he built a sense of dread and gloom. Write a paragraph explaining how Lennie's character flaw, his not being able to control his strength, led to his downfall.

On a separate piece of paper, draw the following chart and give four instances when Lennie couldn't control his strength.

ATMOSPHERE OF DOOM

12. Symbols in *Of Mice and Men*

A symbol is a person, a place, an activity, or an object that stands for something beyond itself. On a separate piece of paper, complete the following symbol chart for the story.

SYMBOL	EXPLAIN WHAT IT REPRESENTS IN THE NOVEL
Western magazines	
Candy's dog	
Curley's wiry hair	
Crook's bare light bulb	
Red slippers and ostrich feathers	

13. The Shooting of Lennie: An Act of Murder or of Mercy?

Although Steinbeck carefully tried to prepare the reader for the shooting of Lennie at the end of the book, the event is still shocking. Answer the following questions in a paragraph.

a. Is George a hero? Did he commit an act of murder or of mercy?
b. Why did George kill Lennie?
c. Was George compassionate in the method he used to kill Lennie?
d. If George did not kill Lennie, what two choices were left for Lennie? Give examples from the book to support the unpleasant outcomes that Lennie would face if George did not kill him. Remember to use at least one direct quote.

14. The Price of a Farm Today

a. **Location**: Decide on a location for your five-acre farm.
b. **Price of land**: Contact a real estate agent in that location. Inquire about the cost of the farm and yearly taxes.
c. **Equipment**: Decide what you will grow on the farm. What equipment will you need to buy? What is the cost of the equipment?
d. **Sowing the land**: How much will it cost to plant your crop (seeds, chemicals, fertilizer)?
e. **Your Comments and Observations**

Romeo and Juliet Project

Choose a book style: Dutch door book, panel book, or explosion book

Supplies: Check the specific book for supplies needed. Fold the worksheets into the book's pockets.

The following topics must be included in your interactive book.

1. Elizabethan Life

Create fifteen trading cards on several aspects of Elizabethan life. Use the Internet to research, summarize, and find pictures to produce fifteen cards.

2. Timeline of Romeo and Juliet

List the events that occur on each day.

3. Common Themes in All Shakespeare Plays

Give examples that demonstrate themes in *Romeo and Juliet*.

- Contrasting worlds (different economic groups)
- Appearance vs. reality
- Desiring that which one cannot have
- Disorder in state or family
- Power of forgiveness

4. Tragic Hero and Tragic Flaw

What is a tragic hero? Which character is a tragic hero? Explain his/her flaw and give one example.

5. Shakespeare's Perspective

What do you think are the author's feelings on these themes?

- Love and hate
- Romance
- Revenge
- Interaction of youth and elders

6. Dramatic and Poetic Terms

Define and give examples of the following:

- Soliloquy
- Aside
- Pun
- Comic relief
- Figurative language
- Oxymoron

7. Duels in Shakespeare's Time

Analyze one fight scene. Consider who duels. Why do these characters duel? What weapons do they use? Who wins?

8. Chance Events

Discuss three events that are ironic and could have happened by chance, coincidence, or accident. Explain why each is unexpected.

9. Choice Events

Explain three events for which Romeo and Juliet are responsible.

10. Love vs. Infatuation

What is the difference between love and infatuation? Are Romeo and Juliet in love or are they infatuated with one another? Defend your position.

11. Foiled Again

Using a Venn diagram, compare and contrast Romeo's two friends, Benvolio and Mercutio. How do they serve as foils for one another?

12. Advice Column

Turn back time and pretend Romeo and Juliet are contemplating a speedy and secretive marriage. What advice could you give to Romeo and Juliet to solve their problem with each other, with their parents, and with their community?

13. The Making of a Comedy

What three events in the play could be changed to make it into a hilarious comedy? (_____ occurs in the play. Instead, have _____ occur.)

14. Map of Italy

Draw a map of Italy and highlight important places in the play. Use the map given out in class.

15. Justice Is Served in Verona

These three characters contributed indirectly to the tragic deaths of Romeo and Juliet. Explain the ways each was involved, if each should be punished, and what that punishment should be.

- The friar
- The nurse
- The apothecary

15. Foreshadowing

A dramatist sometimes uses foreshadowing to suggest coming events. Name three occasions when either Romeo or Juliet had premonitions of disaster.

16. Bad News

Pretend you are a journalist and write a brief article for the *Verona Times Newspaper*. Announce the deaths of Romeo and Juliet. Include an article about the parents' reactions to the death, funeral arrangements, and the building of the statues.

17. Famous Lines

Write at least five lines from the play that are memorable to you. They could be words of wisdom, entertaining lines, or love-filled poetry.

18. Traits of an Ideal Mate

Create a secret handmade envelope in a contrasting color from the book. Inside the letter, write a paragraph describing the personality characteristics of your ideal mate. Seal it with wax to symbolize that this person is perfect (made of wax).

19. Fast Forces of Attraction

Romeo and Juliet meet at the Capulets' masked ball. Explain at least three forces of attraction at work when Romeo and Juliet encounter each other.

20. Television Book Club

You have been invited to appear on a TV show to share your insights and feelings about the play, *Romeo and Juliet*. Write down your thoughts about the play.

Trouble in Paradise
Romeo and Juliet Seek Help from Renowned Psychologist

Problem: We met last night at a party and would like to get married tomorrow, but our parents are feuding. Also, the members of the community are divided by our families' quarrel. Dr. Phil, what should we do?

Paste a photo or draw a picture of yourself here.

Illustrate the lovers, Romeo and Juliet.
(Clip art, drawing or photo)

This is what I suggest you work on with your parents:

This is what I suggest you two work on as a couple:

This is what your community needs from you:

Illustrate the death of Romeo and Juliet.

Justice Is Served in Verona

Friar Drugs Juliet

[Illustration of Friar]

Friar's Involvement:

Families Seek Punishment:

Caption for Photo:

Nurse Linked to Plan

[Illustration of nurse]

Nurse's Involvement:

Families Seek Punishment:

Medical Examiners Reveal Autopsy Findings

Romeo Montague:

Juliet Capulet:

Apothecary Supplies Deadly Poison

[Illustration of bottle of poison]

Apothecary's Involvement:

Families Seek Punishment:

Give the newspaper a clever name
Play with typeface and print size

Drawing of the death of Romeo and Juliet at the scene.

Clever headline explaining parents' reaction to death

Illustration of Capulet

Illustration of Montague

Caption:

Clever headline announcing deaths of Romeo and Juliet

Lead: Paragraph 1: who, what, where, and when.

Paragraph 2: Summarize the tragedy.

Lead: Paragraph 1: who, what, where, and when.

Paragraph 2: Summarize the the parents' reactions to the deaths of their children.

Photo

Funeral arrangements

Future plans

Love vs. Infatuation

Write one paragraph: Analyze the difference between love and infatuation. Which category do you think describes Romeo and Juliet's relationship? Give specific details to back up your answer.

Infatuation

- The relationship is intense, usually short lived, and occupies all your thoughts and energies.
- The physical appearance of your partner is very important.
- Physical attraction is constantly on your mind.
- When you are together, physical contact is a high priority.
- You cannot see faults in the other person.
- You tend to ignore problems and differences.
- You hide many of your faults and weaknesses for fear the other person won't like you.
- The relationship tempts you to compromise your values and beliefs.

Love

- The relationship grows deeper and stronger over time.
- You are able to focus on other areas of your life as well.
- Your partner's personality and character traits are more important than looks.
- You can enjoy being with the other person without physical contact.
- Although you enjoy affection, you also share a courteous, respectful interaction.
- You can recognize strengths as well as weaknesses in one another.
- You recognize problems and differences and work toward resolution.
- You are open and honest with one another and feel safe being your real self.
- The relationship encourages each of you to be a better person and to respect one another's values and beliefs.

Television Book Club

Can you summarize the book for the audience?

Design a new cover for the *Romeo and Juliet* play

What was your favorite part of the book?

What was your learning moment in the book?

Our audience wants to know whether this book is worth reading. Why or why not?

Fast Forces of Attraction

1. Having a pleasant voice: pitch and tone
2. Having a good reputation
3. Being from the same socio-economic class
4. Having a symmetrical face
5. Having a positive mood
6. Being in synchrony with the other person
7. Having confidence and being relaxed; having positive body language
8. Playing hard to get; not being desperate
9. Having a good sense of humor

Romeo and Juliet meet at the Capulets' masked ball. Write one paragraph that explains at least three forces of attraction at work when Romeo and Juliet encounter each other.

Character Traits

A person of great character has several of these traits. Using specific examples from the novel, explain how one character does or does not possess five of the following traits.

CARING: Being kind, helpful, and generous to everyone; caring people are not selfish; they are considerate and always think about how their conduct affects others; they have compassion and empathy; they care how others feel and they are charitable and forgiving; they do good deeds without thought of reward.

COURAGE: Having the determination to do the right thing even when others don't; the strength to follow one's conscience rather than the crowd; attempting difficult things that are worthwhile.

CITIZENSHIP: Doing one's share to help family and make the community a better place; good citizens are good neighbors; they cooperate with others, obey laws and rules, protect the environment, and respect the authority of parents, teachers, and others.

FAIRNESS: Playing by the rules, taking turns, sharing and listening; fair people do not take advantage of others; they consider all sides before they decide and don't blame others unjustly.

GOOD JUDGMENT: Choosing worthy goals and setting proper priorities; thinking through the consequences of one's actions; basing decisions on practical wisdom and good sense.

INTEGRITY: Having the inner strength to be truthful, trustworthy, and honest in all things; acting justly and honorably.

KINDNESS: Being considerate, courteous, helpful, and understanding of others; showing care, compassion, friendship, and generosity; treating others as one would like to be treated.

PERSEVERANCE: Being persistent in pursuit of worthy objectives in spite of difficulty, opposition, or discouragement; exhibiting patience and having the fortitude to try again when confronted with delays, mistakes, or failures.

RESPECT: Showing high regard for authority, for other people, for self, for property, and for country; understanding that all people have value as human beings.

RESPONSIBILITY: Being dependable in carrying out obligations and duties; showing reliability and consistency in words and conduct; being accountable for one's own actions; being committed to active involvement in one's community.

SELF-DISCIPLINE: Demonstrating hard work and commitment to purpose; regulating oneself for improvement and refraining from inappropriate behaviors; being in proper control of one's words, actions, impulses, and desires; choosing abstinence from harmful substances and behaviors; doing one's best in all situations.

TRUSTWORTHINESS: Being honest, telling the truth, keeping promises, and being loyal to earn people's trust; trustworthy people don't lie, cheat, or steal; they have integrity and the moral courage to do the right thing and stand up for their beliefs even when it is hard.

Conflict-resolution Skills

One common element in literature is conflict. By teaching students strategies to analyze and solve conflicts within books, they also learn to transfer this knowledge to their own lives. When children and adults are good problem solvers, they are better able to cope with conflict in their lives and can recognize alternatives to using violence. Teaching win/win resolution skills through role-play conflicts presented in a book helps students find ways to resolve problems productively.

Lesson Objective: Students will become aware of the many factors that interfere with good listening.

Assignment 1

Have students read the following information on conflict resolution and win/win solutions to understand all the barriers to communication that people use. Discuss how this can help in many aspects of life.

Put students in pairs. Ask each pair to choose one of the slips of paper and to prepare a role-play to demonstrate that barrier for the class. Ask the class to guess which barrier was being role-played. Students may discover that all of the items listed are not always barriers and may enhance communication at times. For example, good body language, humor, and physical appearance can improve communication among people. Invite suggestions from students for overcoming the barriers.

BARRIERS TO COMMUNICATION

Lack of concentration	Different importance placed on issues
Different knowledge levels	Body language
Lack of motivation	Lack of commitment
Trigger words and name calling	Disruptive emotions
Cultural differences	Different values
Misunderstandings	Unequal power
Lack of trust	Prejudice
Lecturing	Frequent interruptions
Humor	Physical wellness
Physical appearance	First impressions – prior contacts
Environment	Poor listening skills
Different meanings given to same words	Giving unwanted advice and suggestions

(Adapted from http://disputeresolution.ohio.gov/schools/contentpages/barriers20.htm)

LEARNING TO FIGHT FAIR

1. We find out the problem.
2. We attack the problem, not the person.
3. We listen to each other.
4. We care about each other's feelings.
5. We are responsible for what we say and do.

NO

Foul words	Blaming
Getting even	Hitting
Making excuses	Name calling
Bossing	Not listening
Teasing	Put-downs

HOW TO WORK OUT CONFLICTS FAIRLY AND PEACEFULLY

1. STOP . . .

before you lose control of your temper and make the conflict worse.

2. SAY . . .

what you feel is the problem. What is causing the disagreement? What do you want?

3. LISTEN . . .

to the other person's ideas and feelings.

4. THINK . . .

of solutions that will satisfy both of you.

If you still can't agree, ask someone else to help you work it out.

INFLUENCING FOR WIN/WIN OUTCOMES

Influencing for win/win outcomes takes skill and a collaborative attitude. Before you have an influencing conversation, answer these questions to see if you are in a win/win frame of mind. Are you willing to:

- focus on the question, "How can we both get what we want?" versus "How can I get what I want?"
- really listen to the other person's reactions?
- be flexible about the final result and open to the other person's ideas?
- do at least as much, if not more, than you are asking the other person to do in support of your plan?
- share ownership and credit for results?

Assignment 2

"THE TALK": USING CONFLICT-RESOLUTION SKILLS

What if two characters having a conflict decided to discuss the situation at hand? What conversation would take place?

THE TASK: Choose two characters. Create the conversation that would take place between these individuals if they decided to work things out in a positive way.

THE CRITERIA:

- Explain the situation from each character's point of view
- Incorporate character traits that you already know they have
- The individuals should react in a way that matches what we already know about them from our reading
- Use win/win guidelines from your reading to create a win/win resolution
- Twelve-line minimum (six per speaker)

SPEAKER 1	(Name):	
SPEAKER 2	(Name):	
SPEAKER 1		
SPEAKER 2		
SPEAKER 1		
SPEAKER 2		
SPEAKER 1		
SPEAKER 2		
SPEAKER 1		
SPEAKER 2		
SPEAKER 1		
SPEAKER 2		

Transforming Disaster into Humor

Many works of literature are often serious, with characters experiencing hardships. You are a writer for *Saturday Night Live,* and your task is to transform three elements in the text to make it more amusing. Use the following six types of humor to guide you in your makeover.

HYPERBOLE: Exaggeration or overstatement.
Example: "My dad is as tall as a skyscraper."

UNDERSTATEMENT: Playing down the significance of something; the opposite of hyperbole.
Example: "After my brother totally wrecked his car, he said it was just a little scratch."

IRONY: A usually humorous contrast between what is said and what is meant, what is said and what is done, and what is expected and what occurs.
Example: "My friends say, 'Nice haircut!' after a horrible trip to the beauty salon."

NAIVETY OR MISUNDERSTANDING: Demonstrating innocence or ignorance by making unknowingly humorous comments.
Example: "The little girl asked if the lavatory is a place where they do scientific experiments."

PHYSICAL COMEDY OR SIGHT GAG: An accident in which no one is hurt or a comical physical appearance.
Example: A clown falling off a unicycle or a person dressed as another person.

OVERLY FORMAL LANGUAGE: Using proper or ceremonial speech rather than more common, everyday speech.
Example: "Upon crossing the threshold, a friendly salutation is requested instead of a simple 'Hi.'"

(Adapted from http://library.thinkquest.org/J002267F/types_of_humor.htm)

Bibliography

Andrade, Heidi Goodrich. "Understanding Rubrics." 22 Oct. 2001. <http://www.middleweb.com/rubricsHG.html>.

Audrieth, Anthony L. "Different Types of Verbal and Written Humor." The Art of Using Humor in Public Speaking 1998. Web. 5 Sep. 2009. <http://library.thinkquest.org/J002267F/types_of_humor.htm>.

Bloom B. S. (1956). *Taxonomy of Educational Objectives, Handbook I: The Cognitive Domain*. New York: David McKay Co. Inc.

Charles, Michelle. *Mad for Minis*. 1st. Fort Worth, TX: Design Originals, 2005. Print.

Clark, Don. "Bloom. Big Dog Little Dog's Performance Juxtaposition." May 26, 2009. Knowledge Jump Production. 31 July 2009. <http://www.nwlink.com/~donclark/hrd/bloom.html#reference>.

Garner, Traci. *Designing Writing Assignments*. 1st. Urbana Illinois: National Council of Teachers of English, 2008. Print.

Hall, T. *Differentiated Instruction*. Wakefield, MA: National Center on Accessing the General Curriculum, 2002. http://www.cast.org/publications/ncac/ncac_diffinstruc.html.

"Introduction to Project Based Learning." *Project Based Learning Handbook*. 2007. Bucks Institute for Education. Web. 23 Aug. 2009. <http://www.bie.org/index.php/site/PBL/pbl_handbook_introduction/>.

Johnson, Anne Akers. *Handmade Cards*. 1st. Palo Alto, CA: Klutz, 2003. Print.

Kemper, Dave, Patrick Sebranek, and Verne Meyer. *Write Source*. 1st ed. Wilmington, MA: Houghton Mifflin, 2007. Print.

Librera, Willam L., Ed.D. "New Jersey Core Curriculum Content Standards." *State of New Jersey Department of Education*. 2004. Web. 5 Aug. 2009. <http://education.state.nj.us/cccs>.

Mauk, John, and John Metz. *The Composition of Everyday Life: A Guide to Writing*. 1st ed. Boston, MA: Thomson Wadsworth, 2004. Print.

Mone, Maria L. "Conflict Resolution in Educational Resources." September 2008. *Ohio Common Dispute Resolution and Conflict Management*. 5 Sep. 2009. <http://disputeresolution.ohio.gov/schools.htm>.

Pinecone Press Designers. *Word and Shapes Book*. 1st. Santa Ana, CA: Pinecone Press, 2008. Print.

Smith, Esther K. *How to Make Books*. 1st. New York: Crown Publishing Group, 2007. Print.

Tomlinson, Carol Ann. *How to Differentiate Instruction in Mixed-Ability Classrooms*. 2nd. Alexandria, VA: Association For Supervision and Curriculum Development, 2001. Print.

Truby, Kellene. *The Paper Bag Book*. 1st. Santa Ana, CA: Pinecone Press, 2005. Print.

"Writing Now." *A Policy Research Brief*. 2008. National Council of Teachers of English. Web. 31 July 2009. <http://www.ncte.org/writingnow>.

NOTES

NOTES

NOTES

NOTES

NOTES

NOTES

NOTES

NOTES